The Mindful Consultant

Balancing high performance and emotional wellbeing

By Paul Breslaine

Copyright © 2023 by Paul Breslaine

All rights reserved. No part of this book may be reproduced, distributed, or transmitted in any form or by any means, including photocopying, recording, or other electronic or mechanical methods, without the prior written permission of the author, except in the case of brief quotations embodied in critical reviews and certain other non-commercial uses permitted by copyright law.

Disclaimer

This book is presented solely for educational and informational purposes. While the author has made every effort to verify the accuracy of the information provided in this book, neither the author nor the publisher assumes any responsibility for errors, inaccuracies, or omissions.

The author and publisher disclaim any liability, loss, or risk incurred as a consequence, directly or indirectly, of the use and application of any of the contents of this book.

This book is not intended as a substitute for the advice of professionals in relevant fields. Readers are urged to consult appropriate professionals for any specific questions or issues.

Table of Content

Chapter 1: A Journey into Mindful Consulting 9

Chapter 2: The Science Behind Mindfulness 27

Chapter 3: The Physiology of Mindfulness 42

Chapter 4: Mindful Breathing Techniques 58

Chapter 5: Advanced Techniques for Deep Relaxation 79

Chapter 6: Mindfulness Meditation Practices 97

Chapter 7: Building Emotional Resilience 119

Chapter 8: Mindfulness in Communication 153

Chapter 9: Mindful Leadership 172

Chapter 10: Embracing Mindfulness - Your Path to Professional Excellence 185

Introduction

Welcome to this book on mindfulness and its profound impact on navigating high-pressure, high-performance careers. Whether you're in management consulting, like I have been for over 27 years, or in any demanding profession, this book is for you. My goal is to share insights that can transform your life — without the steep cost of hard-earned lessons that often come with the toll of stress and burnout.

Throughout my career, I've seen firsthand how relentless pressure can leave invisible scars that only manifest later — sometimes in subtle ways, sometimes in painful ones, like anxiety and depression. I remember vividly the day I was driving to a client meeting and suddenly felt short of breath and my vision blurred. I thought I was having a heart attack. I drove straight to the hospital, only to find out it was a panic attack. For years, I'd been burning the candle at both ends, juggling tight deadlines, client expectations, and the relentless pace of consulting.

That day, it had finally caught up with me.

In the consulting world — and many other high-stakes careers — there's rarely room for pause. Whether it's a last-minute request from a client, a compressed timeline to fit a project's budget, or the natural delays that stretch engagements longer than expected, the pressure to deliver is constant. While people can be understanding of personal struggles, the bottom line is that clients expect results. Delivering value below their expectations risks losing them forever, and the consulting industry is nothing if not fiercely competitive.

That's why I had to find a way to manage my anxiety and sustain my performance. A colleague who had gone through a similar experience suggested mindfulness, and while I was initially sceptical, I decided to give it a real try.

It changed everything for me.

For the past 14 years, I've practiced mindfulness, and in these pages, I want to share what I've learned along the way. This isn't an academic book, so I've kept academic references within the text to a minimum. However, I've included research and studies, offering empirical evidence for those who may be sceptical about practices such as mindfulness. I feel that discussing mindfulness from a scientific perspective is important, and full references to these studies can be found at the back of the book for anyone interested in learning more.

Also, meditation, journaling, compassion and gratitude may seem abstract, but they have very real, practical benefits. My hope is that you'll approach this book and these concepts with an open mind. Try even just one practice, and begin to experience the impact it can have on your life.

How to Approach This Book

Although much of what I share stems from my experiences as a management consultant, the principles and practices in this book are relevant to anyone working in high-performance, high-pressure environments (or for anyone who wishes to live a more balanced and mindful life). Whether you're in business, healthcare, education, or any other demanding field, the tools of mindfulness can be transformative. In such roles, the ability to remain calm under pressure, make clear decisions, and maintain emotional balance is critical, and mindfulness can significantly enhance these capabilities.

Mindfulness has become more than just a personal development tool; it's increasingly recognised as a vital skill in today's fast-paced world. Research shows that mindfulness can improve cognitive functioning, enhance emotional intelligence, and boost overall well-being. This is especially true in high-stress environments, where it provides a buffer against burnout, fatigue, and anxiety. While this book is not a comprehensive guide to the science of mindfulness, I've included references to studies that support these claims, which you'll find in the back of the book should you wish to explore them further.

I also want to address a particular audience — men — who might find mindfulness practices initially unfamiliar or even uncomfortable. There's often a perception that mindfulness or meditation is 'soft' or somehow incompatible with high-powered, results-driven work. Yet, some of the most successful leaders in business, sports, and the military have embraced mindfulness, not as a luxury, but as a necessity for sustaining peak performance over the long term. The practice is not about detaching from the world or becoming less competitive; it's about sharpening your focus, managing emotions, and making better decisions under pressure. If you remain open to it, you may discover that mindfulness is less about relaxation and more about building mental resilience.

It's important to approach mindfulness with an open mind. In Zen Buddhism, they speak of 'Shoshin,' or 'beginner's mind,' the practice of approaching each moment with fresh eyes, free from judgement and assumptions. As you go through this book, I encourage you to adopt this perspective. You may come across ideas or techniques that feel unfamiliar or challenging. But if you can maintain that sense of openness, you may be surprised at how effective these practices can be, even in the most intense, high-pressure situations.

This book is intentionally concise, getting to the key takeaways without adding too much fluff. I know time is valuable, especially for people in demanding careers. It should take about three to four hours to read, but I'd like you to think of this time as an investment in your long-term emotional and mental well-being. With your time being valuable in mind, I have purposefully stayed away from writing a chapter on, or delving deeply into the history of mindfulness, which while interesting, I don't think will add much to the key messages I wish to convey.

Whether you take away one powerful idea or several, the insights you gain from these pages will likely stay with you, offering tools you can use again and again as you navigate the challenges of both your professional and personal life.

Incorporating mindfulness into your life is not about making drastic changes overnight. It's a gradual process that, over time, helps you cultivate a deeper sense of self-awareness, balance, and resilience. You might start with a few minutes of mindful breathing each day or learn to check in with your emotions before heading into a difficult meeting. Whatever approach resonates with you, the key is consistency and openness.

So, as you read, stay open to new perspectives. Mindfulness isn't about achieving perfection; it's about learning to meet life with greater presence, compassion, and equanimity. I hope this book provides you with the tools and inspiration to bring more mindfulness into your daily life, allowing you to navigate both the highs and lows with a sense of balance and fulfilment.

Paul Breslaine

Chapter 1: A Journey into Mindful Consulting

> *Be patient with yourself. Self-growth is tender; it's holy ground. There's no greater investment.*
>
> — *Stephen R. Covey*

As a management consultant, you're all too familiar with this scenario: It's 20 minutes before a crucial client meeting, and you're frantically putting the finishing touches on your deck. You're juggling last-minute content development, storyboarding, grammar checks, and formatting while the clock ticks mercilessly.

Your manager's hovering presence only amplifies the pressure (we'll discuss later why this approach is counterproductive). You're sweating profusely, like a turkey on Thanksgiving. Every glance at your watch fills you with dread as the seconds slip away.

Your mind races, conjuring images of the deck becoming corrupted and impacting your mid-year performance review, salary increase, and bonus. The stress is palpable, the anxiety overwhelming.

Sound familiar? This last-minute scramble is an all-too-common experience for many in the consulting world. Trust me, I know; I've been a management consultant for more than

27 years, and it doesn't get easier. No matter how much I plan, get an early start, or delegate effectively, somehow, the last-minute rush is inevitable. It's almost like it should be included in the project plan as a task.

In this fast-paced consulting world, where every moment feels as momentous as the next, there's a way to transform chaos into calm — enter mindfulness. Imagine upgrading from Economy to First Class. That's what integrating mindfulness into your consulting career can feel like. It's not just a trend; it's a powerful shift that can enhance your focus, well-being, and overall effectiveness.

But what is mindfulness, really? Forget the image of shaving your head, wearing an orange robe or sitting cross-legged saying "om" repeatedly. Mindfulness is about being fully present in the moment, aware of your thoughts and emotions, but not controlled by them and not judging them, a concept we'll explore fully a little later.

This chapter is your gateway to discovering how mindfulness can become an indispensable tool in your consulting toolkit, offering everything from stress-relief techniques to strategies that enhance your mental clarity and put your creative and solutions thinking on steroids.

The Origins of Mindfulness

Let's take a quick journey back in time. Mindfulness has deep roots in ancient Buddhist practices developed over 2,500 years ago by Siddhartha Gautama, the Buddha. Originally, these techniques were designed to achieve spiritual enlightenment and alleviate suffering. Fast forward to today, and mindfulness has evolved into something relevant for modern professionals, far removed from its monastic origins. It's a practice that has adapted, much like how we've moved from typewriters to sleek laptops — mindfulness has become a tool as valuable in corporate boardrooms as it once was in monasteries.

In the past few decades, mindfulness has been embraced across various fields — healthcare, education, military and consulting. It is backed by scientific evidence and is used by doctors to manage stress and improve patient care, while teachers introduce it to help students focus and reduce anxiety. This widespread adoption is no coincidence. Mindfulness is the Swiss Army knife of your emotions, versatile and adaptable to different environments and challenges. And for high-stress professionals like you, it's an invaluable tool that can help you maintain focus, build resilience, and navigate the pressures of your career with greater ease.

The Science of Mindfulness in High-Stress Environments

Current and emerging research shows that mindfulness isn't just a feel-good practice — it's grounded in science. Studies have shown that regular mindfulness practice can sharpen attention, enhance decision-making, and boost emotional regulation — all of which are critical skills in consulting. Mindfulness can help reduce cognitive overload and help you stay calm and focused under pressure.

Mindfulness has even found its way into one of the most stressful jobs in the world, being an elite military operator. The U.S. military, including Navy SEALs, has incorporated mindfulness training to enhance its personnel's mental resilience, focus, and stress management. One well-known program is the Mindfulness-Based Mind Fitness Training (MMFT) program, developed by Dr. Elizabeth Stanley. This program has been used to train soldiers and special forces operators to better handle the intense stressors of combat and high-pressure environments, and the benefits are backed by scientific research.

But mindfulness is more than just another stress-relief technique. Unlike meditation, which often focuses on a single point of reference like your breath or a mantra, mindfulness is about maintaining a broad awareness of your thoughts, feelings, and surroundings. This is especially important for people in high-pressure environments who must be alert, focused, and ready to manage multiple responsibilities simultaneously. Understanding this distinction can help you choose the most effective practice for your needs, ensuring that mindfulness becomes a seamless part of your personal and professional life.

From Temples to Boardrooms: The Evolution of Mindfulness

The mindfulness journey from ancient Buddhist temples to modern corporate offices is a testament to its enduring relevance. What began as a spiritual practice to achieve enlightenment has become a practical tool for improved mental clarity and emotional balance. This evolution mirrors mindfulness's core philosophy — cultivating awareness and understanding, whether in a religious or secular context. For you, this means that mindfulness isn't just a passing fad; it's a practice with deep roots and proven benefits, ready to support you in your consulting or any career.

Practical Steps to Integrate Mindfulness into Your Consulting Life

Before you say you're too busy to add mindfulness to your already packed daily schedule, incorporating mindfulness into your daily routine doesn't require drastic changes. Even small practices can make a significant difference, and mindfulness can be practised in almost every moment of your life without needing to sit down and meditate. Before your next meeting, try taking a few moments to practice mindful breathing. This simple act can help calm your mind and prepare you for focused engagement. During stressful moments, pause to observe your thoughts and emotions without getting caught up in them — this can provide clarity and reduce anxiety, making you more effective in your role.

"Sounds good, but how do I observe without engaging my thoughts and emotions?"

Well, I'm glad you asked. A thought is nothing more than a picture or idea that pops up in your mind, helping you understand things and decide what to do.

Without discussing labelling thoughts as "good" or "bad," thoughts alone hold little power. While many people believe in the power of manifestation and visualisation — and I firmly believe that your thoughts shape your mindset and reality, which is key to success — I'm saying that thoughts only gain power when acted upon. This is where mindfulness comes into play, as it allows us to observe our thoughts without judgment and choose which ones to act on deliberately.

The science behind mindfulness further validates its benefits. Neuroimaging studies reveal that regular practice can lead to structural changes in the brain, particularly in areas associated with attention, memory, and emotional regulation. This proves that mindfulness impacts cognitive functions, reinforcing its value for consultants who rely heavily on these skills. By cultivating mindfulness, we can harness the power of our thoughts more effectively, turning them into actionable strategies for personal and professional growth.

Moreover, the emotional benefits, such as reduced anxiety and improved mood, contribute to overall well-being, making it easier to handle the pressures of a demanding career.

The Long-Term Payoff: Sustained Performance and Innovation

But there is a lot more to mindfulness than reducing stress or improving focus in the moment; it's about building a foundation for sustained performance and innovation. Later in the book, I'll discuss the benefits of mindful meditation in accessing altered states of consciousness and how different brainwaves serve different aspects of performance, including creativity and innovation. These profound effects of mindfulness are rooted in the brain's remarkable ability to adapt and change.

Regular mindfulness practice can rewire the brain through a process known as neuroplasticity, enhancing areas responsible for empathy, attention, and emotional regulation. Neuroplasticity is the brain's ability to change and reorganise by forming new neural connections in response to experiences, learning, and behaviours. This biological mechanism underlies the transformative power of mindfulness, allowing practitioners to cultivate lasting improvements in their cognitive and emotional capacities.

For example, studies have shown that consistent mindfulness practice can increase the thickness of the prefrontal cortex (responsible for decision-making and focus) and shrink the amygdala (involved in stress and fear responses), demonstrating how the brain can be physically reshaped through mindfulness. In this sense, mindfulness and neuroplasticity are closely linked, as mindfulness helps trigger and harness the brain's natural capacity to change and adapt.

For consultants, this means becoming more adept at handling future challenges, not just today's problems. It's like continually upgrading your mental hardware and software, making you more resilient, innovative, and effective.

Getting Started with Mindfulness in Consulting

So, how do you begin? Start small. You don't need to meditate for hours; a few minutes of mindful breathing or a short body scan meditation (which will be covered later) can work wonders. Incorporate pauses throughout your day, between meetings, tasks, or even during a coffee break. Take a moment to breathe deeply and check in with yourself. If your organisation doesn't already have one, consider starting a mindfulness group. Having a community can provide support and accountability, making it easier to maintain a regular practice.

Setting Expectations for the Journey Ahead

Embarking on the journey to integrate mindfulness into how you approach your job and life is like setting off on an adventure with excitement and uncertainty. You're not just adding another skill to your toolkit but embracing a transformative process that will unfold over time.

So, let's set the stage with realistic expectations and a clear roadmap.

First, understand that mindfulness isn't a quick fix. It requires ongoing practice that demands patience and commitment. Think of it as planting a seed. You won't see a fully grown tree overnight, but with care and attention, that seed will eventually grow into something strong and resilient. Approaching this journey with a mindset geared towards continuous growth will help you stay motivated and avoid the frustration of expecting instant results.

In her book *Mindset*, Carol Dweck introduces the concept of a growth mindset, which is the belief that abilities and intelligence can be developed through effort and learning. While Dweck's work doesn't explicitly connect this to mindfulness, some researchers and practitioners have drawn parallels between the concepts. Both growth mindset and mindfulness practices can encourage an open awareness of challenges. Mindfulness helps individuals observe their thoughts and emotions without judgment, while a growth mindset can help people view mistakes as opportunities for learning and development rather than failures. This interpretation suggests that combining these approaches might enhance one's ability to face challenges and grow from experiences.

As you start, recognise that mindfulness is about the long game. Just like mastering any other skill, whether learning to storyboard or perfecting how to do MECE (I still haven't), mindfulness requires practice and effort. The benefits of mindfulness accumulate over time, subtly at first but growing more significant as you progress. Another advantage of thinking about mindfulness as a long-term investment is that it shifts your focus from immediate gratification to delaying gratification, which is the deeper and more rewarding process of personal and professional growth.

In *The Road Less Traveled*, M. Scott Peck presents delaying gratification as a fundamental discipline for dealing with life's problems and achieving personal growth. He argues that postponing immediate pleasure for long-term gain is essential for psychological maturity. He contends that this discipline allows people to develop resilience, improve decision-making skills, and ultimately experience greater satisfaction. Peck sees the willingness to delay gratification as a distinguishing factor between those who achieve their goals and those who struggle with life's challenges, suggesting it's a crucial skill for navigating the difficulties and challenges of life.

Adopting a sustainable approach to mindfulness is crucial for those in high-stress environments like consulting, where the pressure can feel relentless. It's about developing a habit that strengthens with time and consistency, like a muscle that grows with regular exercise. As you practice, you might notice small changes — maybe your focus sharpens, or you find yourself handling stress more easily. These subtle shifts are the first signs of something much bigger at play. The seed you planted is starting to show signs of life through the gradual building of resilience, enhanced focus, and overall well-being.

Of course, the path to mindfulness isn't always smooth. There will be ups and downs, days when progress feels slow or non-existent. It's easy to get discouraged during these times but remember that personal or professional growth takes time. When I was seriously training and focused on building muscle, it felt like progress took forever, no matter how hard I trained. However, once I noticed signs of growth, the transformation felt rapid — until I hit a plateau. Then the cycle would start again, from a much higher baseline each time. I found the same when building my mindfulness practice. Patience is your ally here. Instead of fixating on the end goal, embrace each step as part of the learning process. Every challenge is an opportunity for deeper self-awareness and improvement.

As we progress in this journey, we'll explore key themes and practices designed to enrich your professional and personal life. Future chapters will introduce you to techniques like focused breathing, mindful listening, and other practical exercises tailored specifically for the consulting world. These offer just a glimpse of the transformative potential that lies ahead, igniting excitement and preparing you for what's to come.

Committing to at least one technique that resonates with you is important to successfully integrate mindfulness into your life. This commitment becomes the cornerstone of your practice, instilling a sense of ownership and accountability for your journey. Whether setting aside a few minutes each day for meditation or practising mindful breathing during hectic moments, choosing a technique that feels natural to you increases the likelihood that you'll stick with it.

Incorporating mindfulness into your daily routine should not feel like a chore. It's about finding what works for you and making it part of your day in a way that feels sustainable. You might start with short, focused sessions and gradually extend them as you become more comfortable. Or perhaps you'll find it helpful to pair mindfulness practices with existing routines — like practising mindful breathing during your commute or eating breakfast.

In the beginning, practising mindfulness might feel awkward or challenging, much like any new habit. But just as physical fitness improves with regular exercise, so will your mental clarity and emotional resilience strengthen with consistent mindfulness practice. It's normal to initially encounter resistance or discomfort, but pushing through these initial barriers can lead to profound growth and a greater ability to handle stress.

Don't forget the value of seeking support along the way. Connecting with peers who have experience with mindfulness or sharing your journey with others can be valuable in keeping you motivated. It also helps to remind you that you're not alone in this, creating a sense of community and shared purpose.

Implementing Mindfulness in Consulting Practices

Let's discuss how you can bring mindfulness into your daily consulting work.

One simple yet powerful strategy is integrating mindfulness exercises like focused breathing and mindful listening into your daily meetings or client interactions. For instance, take a few deep breaths before walking into a meeting. This small act can clear your mind, reduce anxiety, and set a calm tone for the encounter. Similarly, practising mindful listening (or, as some people call it, active listening) — fully concentrating on the speaker without letting your mind wander — can vastly improve communication. When you're truly present, your clients will notice, and they'll feel more valued and understood.

Another critical step is developing a personal mindfulness routine that suits your lifestyle. It doesn't have to be lengthy; even five minutes of meditation each morning can make a difference. Consider starting with a simple practice like the "Observer Meditation," where you adopt an observer's perspective, focusing on physical sensations and emotions without judgment. When we say without judgment, it is basically observing your thoughts, feelings, and sensations without labelling them as good or bad, right or wrong, and accepting experiences as they are, without reacting to them emotionally or critically (more about this later).

This approach helps you gain insight into your mental state, setting a clear and composed tone for the day ahead.

Integrating these strategies into your busy schedule might seem challenging initially, but the long-term benefits make it well worth the effort. Simple exercises like focused breathing or mindful listening don't require much time but can profoundly impact your stress levels and cognitive function. A consistent personal routine helps maintain a steady mental state, which is vital for making sound decisions under pressure.

The Role of the Firm

Consulting firms can also play a significant role by introducing mindfulness training programs or workshops. These could include sessions on mindful leadership, stress reduction techniques, or even mindfulness retreats. Such initiatives foster a culture of mindfulness, encouraging collective practice that enhances team cohesion and overall performance. For example, programs like Mindfulness-Based Stress Reduction (MBSR) have significantly reduced stress and anxiety, leading to improved productivity and employee morale.

Cultivating a mindfulness culture within your consulting firm ensures mindfulness becomes a shared practice rather than an isolated effort. This supportive environment encourages employees to prioritise their mental health and professional responsibilities. Training sessions and workshops equip staff with essential skills and demonstrate the organisation's commitment to their well-being.

Systematic evaluation of mindfulness practices ensures that these initiatives continue to grow and evolve. By collecting and analysing feedback, firms can adapt their mindfulness programs to better meet the needs of their employees, reinforcing the idea that growth and development are ongoing processes and that the company is truly invested in their employee's mental and physical wellness.

Integrating mindfulness into your consulting practice and career is a journey of continuous growth. By setting realistic expectations, adopting sustainable practices, and committing to the ongoing nature of mindfulness, you can enhance your focus, reduce stress, and create a healthier work-life balance. Remember, every small step counts each moment of mindfulness contributes to a more resilient and effective professional life and workforce.

Key Takeaways

As we've explored throughout this chapter, integrating mindfulness can be a transformative journey, offering numerous benefits for both personal well-being and professional effectiveness. Let's recap the key points:

- Origins and Evolution: Mindfulness has evolved from ancient Buddhist practices to a scientifically backed tool relevant in modern professional settings, including high-stress environments like consulting and even military operations.
- Benefits for Consultants:
    - Enhanced focus and attention
    - Improved stress management and emotional regulation
    - Better decision-making capabilities
    - Increased resilience and adaptability
    - Potential for greater creativity and innovation
- Scientific Backing: Neuroimaging studies show that regular mindfulness practice can lead to structural changes in the brain, particularly in areas associated with attention, memory, and emotional regulation.
- Practical Integration:

- Start small with brief mindful breathing exercises or short meditations
- Incorporate mindful pauses throughout your workday
- Practice mindful listening during client interactions
- Consider establishing a mindfulness group within your organisation
- **Long-term Perspective:** Approaching mindfulness as a long-term investment rather than a quick fix is crucial. Benefits accumulate over time, leading to sustained performance improvements and personal growth.
- **Organisational Role:** Consulting firms can support this journey by introducing mindfulness training programs, workshops, or retreats, fostering a culture that values mental well-being alongside professional achievement.

Remember, the path to mindfulness is unique for everyone. It requires patience, commitment, and a growth mindset. As you continue to integrate these practices into your consulting life, you may find that your professional effectiveness improves, and you develop a greater sense of balance, clarity, and purpose in your work.

By embracing mindfulness, you're not just enhancing your consulting toolkit — you're investing in a more resilient, focused, and innovative version of yourself. This investment will serve you well throughout your career and life, helping you navigate the challenges of consulting with greater ease and effectiveness.

As you move forward, consider which mindfulness practices resonate most with you and commit to incorporating them into your daily routine. The journey of mindfulness is ongoing, but with each mindful moment, you're building a foundation for sustained success and well-being in your professional life.

Chapter 2: The Science Behind Mindfulness

You should sit in meditation for twenty minutes every day — unless you're too busy. Then you should sit for an hour

— Zen proverb

One of the things that attracted me to mindfulness and meditation was that it is backed up by scientific evidence. I'm fundamentally sceptical about things that are not mainstream, but I'm always happy to do research and become a believer if the research pans out.

My first experience with Buddhism, mindfulness, and meditation happened in my early twenties. I had developed an interest in Buddhism and wanted to learn more, so my stepdad and I decided to visit a monastery for a 48-hour stay, where we would experience life as monks.

Upon arrival, we were informed that for the next 48 hours, we were not allowed to speak to fully immerse ourselves in the monastic life. Shortly after being shown to our room, we were called for the first meditation session, which involved silently walking around a room while focusing on each step we took. It wasn't exactly as exciting as it sounds. After what felt like 10,000 steps of literally going around in circles, we finally stopped for tea — called Fuquan — that tasted like lukewarm dishwater.

Next, we were ushered into a room for sitting meditation. This is where things got interesting. The monk leading the meditation spoke with a strong accent, and I struggled to understand him. Everyone else seemed to follow along just fine, eyes closed, deep in meditation. But I sat there, looking at the monk, clearly confused, likely with a blank or puzzled expression. The monk, noticing me staring at him, said, "Don't look me," in a somewhat displeased voice.

I closed my eyes, resisting the urge to slap a monk for being rude, which I figured wasn't the best way to handle things. Long story short, I convinced my stepdad to leave after supper. So, my first encounter with mindfulness and meditation lasted less than four hours. To this day, my stepdad still jokes that I'm the only person he knows who managed to offend a Buddhist monk.

Mindfulness might seem like just another trendy buzzword, but its influence reaches deep into the very core of our brains. How crazy is it that by simply sitting quietly and focusing on your breath, you can reshape the structure of your brain? That's right — mindfulness isn't just for monks meditating on mountaintops; it's a scientifically validated practice that can help even the most overwhelmed professionals find their inner calm.

This chapter will explore how mindfulness physically alters the brain, enhancing functions critical to personal well-being and professional success. We'll examine studies showing increased grey matter in areas responsible for growth and emotional health. You'll also discover how mindfulness strengthens the connections between key brain regions, leading to better decision-making and stress management. Plus, through consistent mindfulness practice, we'll delve into the brain's incredible ability to rewire itself — thanks to the magic of neuroplasticity.

So, get ready to journey through the neural pathways and see how just a few mindful minutes a day can transform your brain and supercharge your professional prowess.

Neuroscience of Mindfulness

In high-stress environments where decisions must be sharp and leadership steady, mindfulness is more than just a calming practice — it's a powerful tool that can physically reshape the brain to enhance performance.

Let's start with some brain science. Regular mindfulness practice has been shown to increase grey matter in key brain regions associated with learning, memory, and emotional regulation. Think of this as giving your brain a workout, building up the areas that support cognitive functioning, mental resilience, and emotional intelligence. For instance, the hippocampus, a region critical for learning and memory, shows significant growth with consistent mindfulness practice. A 2011 landmark study by Britta Hölzel and her colleagues found that participants who completed an eight-week mindfulness program saw measurable increases in grey matter density, particularly in regions related to emotional regulation. For professionals navigating complex and high-pressure environments, these enhancements are like upgrading the brain's operating system to handle life's demands more efficiently.

Mindfulness also improves the brain's connectivity, particularly between the prefrontal cortex (responsible for executive functions like decision-making) and the amygdala (which processes emotions). Strengthening this connection means better control over your emotional responses and more strategic decision-making.

Another fascinating aspect of mindfulness is its role in promoting neuroplasticity — the brain's ability to adapt and reorganise itself. Mindfulness encourages this flexibility, allowing your brain to form new neural connections and pathways. This adaptability is crucial for professionals who must recover quickly from setbacks, embrace a growth mindset, and remain effective in dynamic, demanding fields.

Consider how we develop new habits and break old ones. Neuroplasticity involves strengthening frequently used neural pathways and pruning less-used ones (synaptic plasticity). When developing a habit, repeated behaviours strengthen specific neural circuits, making the habit automatic over time. Conversely, breaking a habit requires weakening the existing neural connections through continuous inaction while forming new pathways.

Neuroplasticity and habit formation are like rivers carving a path. Repeated behaviours strengthen neural pathways, like continuous water flow which carves a new path through the rock. As more water flows through this new path, the old channel starts to dry up, and eventually, no more water goes through it, while the new path deepens and gets stronger.

Mindfulness also plays a key role in calming the amygdala, the part of the brain central to our experience of fear and stress. By decreasing the amygdala's reactivity, mindfulness helps you manage stress more efficiently and prevents emotional escalations. This translates into a calmer, more measured approach to problem-solving, ensuring that you respond thoughtfully rather than react impulsively — a critical distinction in professional and personal interactions. But more about this in Chapter 3.

Beyond these direct effects, mindfulness also enhances cognitive control and emotional regulation. It improves attention regulation, allowing you to stay focused and avoid distractions during tasks. Moreover, mindfulness strengthens inhibitory control, the ability to suppress unwanted thoughts and impulses. This skill is particularly valuable when making well-considered decisions under pressure, helping you maintain composure and think clearly in high-stakes situations.

The benefits of mindfulness extend even further to the anterior cingulate cortex (ACC), a brain area involved in self-regulation and mental flexibility. Mindfulness practitioners show increased activity in the ACC, which aids in handling impulsivity and adapting to new information or changing environments. For professionals, you're better equipped to pivot quickly and make informed decisions even when under pressure.

Mindfulness and Stress Reduction

Stress is often a constant companion in the high-octane consulting world and other demanding professions. However, mindfulness is a powerful counterbalance to help manage and reduce that stress.

One of the most compelling aspects of mindfulness is its impact on cortisol levels, the body's primary stress hormone. Elevated cortisol over time can wreak havoc on your health, leading to impaired cognitive function, a weakened immune system, and an increased risk of mental health disorders. A study by Rogerson, Wilding, and Prudenzi showed that mindfulness practices significantly lower cortisol levels, contributing to better physical health and enhanced cognitive performance. For professionals, this stress reduction is pivotal to avoiding burnout, maintaining productivity, and staying resilient in competitive environments.

The long-term benefits of mindfulness on stress reduction are well-documented. Professionals who participate in mindfulness programs consistently report lower stress levels, with these positive effects lasting over time. Janssen et al suggests that mindfulness offers immediate relief and contributes to sustained improvements in mental well-being and overall organisational health. Additionally, mindfulness empowers you to manage stress independently, fostering confidence, self-reliance, and an internal sense of control, allowing you to navigate complex situations with greater composure and clarity.

Cognitive Benefits: Focus and Concentration

Let's briefly explore how mindfulness can sharpen focus and concentration — two essential skills when the pressure is on.

Imagine you're standing at a critical crossroads in your workday. Data are flooding in from multiple sources, colleagues are chatting around you, and your inbox keeps pinging with new emails. Your brain feels like it's juggling flaming swords while you are blindfolded, trying to balance on a unicycle. This is where mindfulness steps in as your mental superhero. A study by Hodgins and Adair showed that consistent mindfulness practice significantly improves attention span and concentration. For example, according to the research, dedicated meditators are less distracted by irrelevant cues than those who don't practice mindfulness. While Wimmer et al contends this heightened focus enables deeper analysis, creative problem-solving, and significantly reduced errors — transforming chaos into manageable order.

The ability to zero in on what truly matters while filtering out distractions is essential in demanding environments. Mindfulness teaches you how to reduce cognitive distractions. Picture this: instead of being pulled in every direction, your mind remains anchored, allowing you to maintain high productivity and make clear decisions. Think of it as having noise-cancelling headphones for your brain, muting the unnecessary mental chatter so you can stay focused on the task at hand.

Another powerful benefit of mindfulness is its enhancement of working memory capacity. Working memory is like a mental whiteboard where you temporarily jot down and manipulate information. It's crucial for juggling multiple responsibilities without dropping the ball. Studies like the one conducted by Chiesa, Calati, and Serretti show that mindfulness-based training improves performance in tasks requiring working memory, enabling professionals to simultaneously keep track of numerous projects and details.

Extensive research underscores these cognitive benefits. Multiple studies link mindfulness practices to significant improvements in cognitive function, providing a solid basis for individuals and organisations to adopt mindfulness. These findings highlight that mindfulness isn't just a trendy wellness fad; it's a scientifically supported strategy for boosting mental acuity and efficiency in high-pressure scenarios.

For employers and team leaders, fostering mindfulness within organisations enhances individual performance and elevates overall team dynamics. Teams that engage in mindfulness training are likely to experience fewer interpersonal conflicts, better collaboration, and higher innovation rates. A calm and collected workforce can navigate complex challenges effectively, driving organisational success.

Emotional Regulation Through Mindfulness

Mindfulness also plays a crucial role in enhancing emotional regulation, an essential skill for high-performing professionals. By becoming more aware of your emotional triggers and reactions, you can foster proactive emotional regulation, leading to thoughtful responses rather than impulsive reactions. This heightened awareness allows you to navigate interpersonal relationships more effectively, creating smoother interactions and reducing conflicts.

Understanding your emotional triggers is like learning a new language — challenging but immensely rewarding. Mindfulness practices, such as meditation and mindful breathing, help you recognise these triggers as they arise. For instance, during a heated meeting or when facing a tight deadline, a professional who has cultivated mindfulness can identify rising anxiety or frustration. Instead of reacting hastily, they can take a mindful pause, allowing them to respond thoughtfully. This approach not only diffuses potential conflicts but also promotes a culture of understanding and patience within the workplace.

Mindfulness also plays a significant role in cultivating empathy and emotional intelligence in professional settings and enhances these qualities. Empathy involves understanding and sharing the feelings of others, which is needed for building strong team dynamics and effective collaboration. Emotional intelligence, the ability to perceive, control, and evaluate emotions, is a core competency for leadership effectiveness. Mindfulness teaches you to be present and fully engaged in interactions, improving your ability to empathise with colleagues' perspectives and emotions.

For example, leaders who practice mindfulness might notice subtle non-verbal cues indicating a team member's distress. With this awareness, they can address issues before they escalate, fostering a supportive environment. Teams with high emotional intelligence are better equipped to handle challenges collaboratively, improving productivity and morale.

In his book *Emotional Intelligence*, Daniel Goleman suggests that while Intelligence Quotient (IQ) is important for cognitive tasks, Emotional Intelligence (EQ) skills like self-awareness, empathy, emotional regulation, and social interaction — play a critical role in managing emotions, fostering collaboration, and achieving long-term success in various areas of life. Goleman argues that EQ is often more important than IQ in determining success, particularly in personal and professional relationships. This is a particularly important insight in consulting, as management consults are typically highly educated and intelligent, both often being table stakes just to enter the game, and therefore considered to be already present.

In the consulting world, I have met some of the smartest and educated people I know — many with incredible knowledge, insights, and an exceptional grasp of their subject matter. However, some of these individuals leave much to be desired when it comes to engaging with others and communicating effectively. This isn't to say that these people are at fault in their communication, but a mindful approach can work wonders in these situations.

Mindfulness is not a one-way street.

When you encounter someone who is brilliant but perhaps socially awkward or lacks strong communication skills, you can improve the interaction by being present, truly listening, and having the courage to ask clarifying questions when needed.

Another significant benefit of mindfulness is its ability to equip you with coping tools for building resilience when faced with emotional challenges. Resilience involves bouncing back from setbacks and maintaining mental well-being despite adversity. Mindfulness practices offer techniques, including grounding exercises and body scans, which help manage stress and prevent burnout.

Imagine a scenario where an engagement fails to meet a critical deadline. A mindful professional would acknowledge their disappointment or frustration without becoming overwhelmed. They would use mindfulness techniques to centre themselves, gaining clarity and perspective. This resilience enables quicker recovery from setbacks, allowing them to return to tasks with renewed focus and determination.

Enhanced emotional regulation through mindfulness leads to more balanced and rational decision-making. Emotional regulation helps you avoid decision fatigue — a mental exhaustion caused by numerous decisions — and reduces emotional bias, ensuring choices are made based on logic and reason rather than transient emotions.

Key Takeaways

In Chapter 2 we looked at some scientific evidence underpinning mindfulness and its profound impact on the brain and cognitive functions. Let's recap the key insights:

- Neuroplasticity and Brain Structure:
    - Mindfulness practice physically reshapes the brain, increasing grey matter in areas associated with learning, memory, and emotional regulation.

- o It strengthens connections between key brain regions, particularly between the prefrontal cortex and amygdala, enhancing decision-making and emotional control.
- o Regular practice promotes neuroplasticity, allowing for greater adaptability and resilience in dynamic professional environments.
- Stress Reduction:
    - o Mindfulness significantly lowers cortisol levels, reducing the negative impacts of chronic stress.
    - o It offers immediate relief and long-term improvements in mental well-being and stress management.
- Cognitive Enhancement:
    - o Practitioners show improved focus, concentration, and working memory capacity.
    - o Mindfulness helps filter out distractions, allowing deeper analysis and more effective problem-solving.
- Emotional Regulation:
    - o Mindfulness cultivates greater awareness of emotional triggers and reactions.
    - o It enhances empathy and emotional intelligence, which are required for effective leadership and team dynamics.

- Mindfulness equips individuals with coping tools, building resilience and enabling quicker recovery from setbacks.
- Decision-Making:
  - By promoting emotional balance, mindfulness leads to more rational and effective decision-making.
  - It helps prevent decision fatigue and reduces emotional bias in high-pressure situations.

The scientific evidence supporting mindfulness is compelling, demonstrating its potential to transform individual performance and entire organisational cultures. By incorporating mindfulness practices into your professional life, you're not just adopting a trendy wellness technique – you're leveraging a scientifically validated tool for enhancing cognitive function, emotional intelligence, and overall well-being.

As we move forward, consider how you might integrate mindfulness into your daily routine. Whether through brief meditation sessions, mindful breathing exercises, or simply taking mindful pauses throughout your day, each moment of practice contributes to rewiring your brain for greater resilience, focus, and emotional balance.

Remember, mindfulness is an ongoing journey. Like any skill, its benefits grow with consistent practice. By committing to mindfulness, you're investing in a more capable, balanced, and effective version of yourself — one that's well-equipped to thrive in the demanding world of consulting and beyond.

Chapter 3: The Physiology of Mindfulness

The mind is just like a muscle—the more you exercise it, the stronger it gets and the more it can expand.

— *Idowu Koyenikan*

Earlier, I mentioned two powerful aspects of mindfulness: enhanced creativity and innovation through altered states of consciousness and learning to respond thoughtfully to situations rather than impulsively reacting. These concepts are not just interesting side notes but powerful tools that deserve their own chapter.

It's important to remember that the brain is incredibly complex, and our understanding of how it works is still evolving. The concepts in this chapter are based on current research, but since science is always advancing, the findings discussed here should be seen as current thinking rather than absolute truths.

Ok, let's dive into these altered states and the art of response, exploring how mindfulness can influence brainwave activity and reshape how we engage with the world.

Altered States of Consciousness

When we talk about altered states of consciousness in mindfulness, we're referring to how meditation and mindfulness practices can help access and influence different brainwave states. Humans experience five distinct brainwave frequencies: Delta, Theta, Alpha, Beta, and Gamma. Each plays a crucial role in how we perceive and interact with the world around us.

Delta Waves

Frequency: 0.5 to 4 Hz

Delta waves, the slowest of all brainwaves, are most prominent during deep, restorative sleep. They are responsible for healing and regeneration — vital for our immune system, cellular repair, and brain recovery. These waves dominate when our body is in its deepest, most restful state, particularly during non-REM sleep stages 3 and 4. This period supports physical and cognitive restoration, making it critical for overall well-being.

To access delta waves through meditation, practices like Yoga Nidra and other deep relaxation techniques are key. These practices promote profound stillness, helping your body and mind reach a state similar to deep sleep. Long-term meditators often show enhanced delta wave activity, allowing them to tap into these restorative benefits even while awake

Theta Waves

Frequency: 4 to 8 Hz

Theta waves are where creativity, intuition, and emotional processing flourish. These waves are most active during light sleep, deep relaxation, and moments of insight, like those 'aha' moments that hit when you least expect it. These waves are particularly prominent during stage 1 and stage 2 sleep, which are lighter stages of sleep. Theta waves play a pivotal role in memory retention, emotional healing, and creativity by helping the brain process and organise information.

Theta waves, are often linked to moments of profound insight, especially in states just before falling asleep. This is why you might have a brilliant idea right before drifting off. Theta waves create the conditions for fluid, abstract thinking, helping the brain solve problems creatively and intuitively.

When I get an epiphany as I'm drifting off to sleep, I prefer not to take physical notes, as it disrupts my ability to relax. However, I do have Alexa, which allows me to quickly dictate a note without interrupting my sleep process too much.

Accessing theta waves through meditation can be achieved through guided visualisations, deep relaxation techniques like body scans, or mindful breathing. These methods allow your brain to disengage from everyday life's logical, focused tasks, opening the door to creative and intuitive thinking. We may also experience theta states during hypnotherapy or deep relaxation, where the subconscious mind can bring forward insights, we may not be aware of in our everyday waking state.

Alpha Waves

Frequency: 8 to 12 Hz

Alpha waves sit in that sweet spot between deep relaxation and alertness, often appearing when the mind is at rest but awake. Think of those moments when you're daydreaming, quietly reflecting, or even just closing your eyes for a brief break — alpha waves are likely at work. They promote a balanced, calm, and focused mental state, helping to reduce stress and anxiety while fostering creativity and problem-solving.

Have you ever had your best ideas while in the shower? That's not a coincidence! When doing something routine or relaxing, like showering, your brain often shifts into an alpha or theta wave state. This state is conducive to creative thinking because it lowers the brain's inhibitory control, allowing thoughts to flow more freely.

Alpha waves dominate when we're relaxed but awake, like during daydreaming or light meditation. In this state, the brain is likelier to make novel connections between ideas, fostering creativity. Studies, such as Fink & Neubauer, have shown that higher alpha wave activity correlates with better creative task performance. So, the next time you need a breakthrough idea, it might be worth swapping that intense brainstorming session for something more laid-back — daydreaming or light reflection might lead to the innovation you seek.

I found it useful to have a pen and paper next to me while meditating so that if I hit a "eureka" moment I can quickly write it down before resuming my meditation.

Practices like breath awareness, body scanning, and mindful walking stimulate alpha wave activity. The key is cultivating a relaxed yet alert state of mind — focusing on the present without becoming distracted.

It's worth mentioning that while research suggests a link between certain brain states and creativity, our understanding of this complex relationship is still evolving, and scientific investigation is ongoing. Additionally, individual experiences with creativity can vary significantly.

Beta Waves

Frequency: 12 to 30 Hz

Beta waves are your go-to for active thinking, decision-making, and problem-solving. Beta waves dominate when you're focused on a task, analysing data, or managing multiple responsibilities. They help keep the brain alert, facilitating concentration and logical thinking, which is crucial in professions that demand precision and cognitive engagement.

While alpha and theta waves open the door to creativity, beta waves ensure you stay sharp and focused when it's time to analyse and execute. In consulting, beta waves are vital. They kick into gear when processing complex information, making decisions, and solving problems. When fully engaged in critical thinking or analysing data, beta waves keep you focused and alert, facilitating logical, structured thought.

Balancing beta wave activity with alpha and theta waves can be a game-changer for consultants. Beta waves are necessary for tasks requiring precision and focus, but too much beta activity without moments of relaxation can lead to mental fatigue.

Mindfulness helps manage this balance, enhancing beta waves for focused work while using practices like breath awareness to prevent stress from taking over. In mindfulness practice, beta waves are regulated through focused attention meditation, where you concentrate on a single object, like your breath or a mantra. This helps harness the benefits of beta wave activity while preventing mental overload.

Gamma Waves

Frequency: 30 to 100 Hz

Gamma waves are the fastest brainwaves, linked to peak cognitive performance, learning, and memory recall. Advanced meditators, especially those practising deep compassion meditations, often exhibit heightened gamma wave activity. Gamma waves are associated with moments of heightened perception and insight, helping integrate information across different parts of the brain.

Gamma brainwaves, which oscillate at a frequency of 30–100 Hz, are thought to be associated with heightened states of cognitive functioning, including happiness, compassion, and peak mental performance. Research suggests that these waves play a role in information processing and conscious awareness, and some studies have linked elevated gamma activity with positive emotional states.

Matthieu Ricard, a 69-year-old Tibetan Buddhist monk, has been dubbed the "happiest man alive" due to his exceptionally high levels of gamma wave activity observed during meditation on compassion. Neuroscientists, including Richard Davidson at the University of Wisconsin-Madison, conducted studies using EEG scans and found that Ricard's brain exhibited an unprecedented level of gamma wave activity, particularly when he engaged in compassion meditation. This suggests a potential link between long-term meditation practice, heightened gamma wave activity, and sustained states of happiness and well-being.

Practices like loving-kindness (metta) meditation or intensive mindfulness practices can stimulate gamma wave activity. These heightened awareness and focus states contribute to a deeper sense of well-being, emotional control, and cognitive clarity.

Practical Integration

Incorporating these brainwave insights into daily consulting life doesn't have to be complicated. Small, regular mindfulness practices can enhance both your creativity and analytical skills. Take breaks to daydream or relax, allowing your brain to enter alpha and theta states for creative insights. When it's time to focus, use mindfulness techniques to stay sharp and engaged, harnessing beta wave activity without letting stress overwhelm you.

By understanding and working with your brain's natural rhythms, you can optimise your performance — whether generating creative ideas or diving deep into complex problem-solving

Mindfulness is a tool for managing stress and accessing altered states of consciousness that boost creativity, focus, and overall mental clarity. As you develop your mindfulness practice, you'll discover how to balance these brainwave states to enhance your well-being and professional effectiveness.

Cortical Inhibition: Why Pressure Hampers Performance

Remember when I mentioned earlier that your manager hovering over your shoulder, piling on the pressure to finish your work, is counterproductive? Well, now it's time to dive into the science behind that. The concept we're looking at here is called cortical inhibition, and it's a key reason why stress can impair your ability to think clearly and make good decisions.

Cortical Inhibition: The Brain's Emergency Shutdown

Cortical inhibition refers to the process by which the brain, especially the prefrontal cortex — responsible for higher-order thinking, decision-making, and emotional regulation — goes into "low-power" mode under stress. This happens because of our body's natural fight-or-flight response, which is triggered by the limbic system, particularly the amygdala when a threat is detected.

Now, the prefrontal cortex is where your reasoning, problem-solving, and emotional control reside. So, why would the brain want to shut down this crucial part, especially when it feels like you need it the most?

The answer lies in our evolutionary wiring.

The Limbic System: Our Ancient Survival Brain

The limbic system is a group of brain structures that help control emotions, behaviour, and long-term memory. It's different from what is sometimes called the "reptilian brain," which refers to older parts of the brain like the brainstem and cerebellum. These older parts are responsible for basic functions like breathing and movement control. The limbic system, which includes the amygdala, hippocampus, and hypothalamus, evolved later and is found in all mammals. It plays a key role in emotions and memory.

Back in the good days when our ancestors faced life-threatening situations — like, say, a rabid ground sloth called Sid — our brain needed to act fast. The amygdala would sound the alarm, triggering the body's fight-or-flight response. There's no time to overanalyse the situation or debate your options in this kind of emergency. You need to act — now! Your body doesn't want higher-order thinking slowing things down, so it "overrides" the prefrontal cortex to conserve energy for more immediate survival functions.

The amygdala signals the hypothalamus to release stress hormones, preparing the body for action by directing energy to your muscles while suppressing non-essential functions like deep cognitive processes. This is cortical inhibition at work. Since the brain uses around 25% of the body's energy despite making up only 2% of its mass, temporarily reducing the energy needs of the prefrontal cortex is a way to conserve resources and improve the odds of survival. In a split-second emergency, complex thought can be more of a liability than an asset.

While there is a lot of research supporting this, it's worth noting that this energy conservation theory has yet to be definitively proven.

Why This Matters in Today's Workplace

Fast forward to today: chances are you're not running from a sabre toothed tiger in the office, but your body doesn't know the difference between a literal life-or-death situation and your manager breathing down your neck or looming deadlines. The limbic system treats both scenarios as threats, triggering the same stress response, including inhibiting your prefrontal cortex. In modern work settings, this means that under stress, your ability to think critically, make decisions, or solve problems is impaired.

When pressure builds and stress kicks in, your brain shifts into survival mode, so you might struggle to focus or feel like you're "going blank" in a tense situation. Rather than helping you finish that report faster, your manager's pressure decreases your cognitive functioning, making you less efficient.

So, the next time this happens, you can tell your manager there is scientific evidence suggesting they are part of the problem and not the solution (although you may want to use nicer words).

The Role of Mindful Breathing: A Pathway to Calm and Clarity

So, how do you counteract this stress-induced shutdown of the prefrontal cortex? Enter mindful breathing, a practice that helps to restore balance and bring your brain back to full capacity. The key player here is the vagus nerve, part of the parasympathetic nervous system — also known as the "rest-and-digest" system.

When you engage in mindful breathing, particularly slow and deep breaths, you activate the vagus nerve, which slows down your heart rate and promotes relaxation. This activation puts the brakes on the fight-or-flight response initiated by the amygdala. By engaging the vagus nerve, mindful breathing calms the limbic system, reduces amygdala activity, and helps restore energy flow to the prefrontal cortex.

This process creates coherence between the brain, heart, and body — a synchronised, balanced state where all physiological systems work in harmony. In this state, your cognitive abilities return, allowing you to think more clearly, regulate your emotions better, and make thoughtful decisions, even in stressful situations.

If you want to see this process in action, I recommend watching Alan Watkins' TEDx talk, "Being Brilliant Every Single Day." In it, he discusses the science of coherence and how it can transform one's ability to perform under pressure and gives a physical demonstration of how stress can inhibit cognitive functioning.

So, what's the takeaway for the workplace? The next time your manager applies pressure, remember that the stress you feel might be inhibiting the part of your brain you need to get the job done. Mindful breathing can help you recover from this reactive state, re-engaging the prefrontal cortex to allow for calm, clear thinking. When under pressure, stepping away to focus on your breath for even a minute or two can re-establish balance and restore your cognitive abilities.

Understanding how your brain works under stress is a game-changer. It shows that high-pressure tactics aren't just unpleasant — they're counterproductive. By promoting mindfulness and stress-reducing techniques in the workplace, individuals and organisations can ensure better decision-making, improved emotional regulation, and overall higher performance.

Why You Go Blank During Exams (and Other Stressful Moments)

On a side note, the same physiological process explains why some students experience going "blank" during exams, even when they've studied diligently. Exam stress triggers the fight-or-flight response, which leads to cortical inhibition of the prefrontal cortex — the part of the brain responsible for reasoning and recall. The information is in there somewhere, but the brain is too busy reacting to perceived danger to let you access it.

This doesn't mean the student didn't prepare well. It's simply that their body's stress response has temporarily hijacked their brain's higher-order functions. In such cases, poor performance doesn't reflect knowledge and understanding but rather stress management. Mindfulness for students can be a game changer.

Key Takeaways

Throughout this chapter, we've looked at the intricate relationship between mindfulness practices and brain function, particularly focusing on brainwave states and our evolutionary wiring, and their impact on creativity, focus, and stress response. Let's recap the key insights:

- Brainwave States and Their Functions:
    - Delta (0.5-4 Hz): Deep sleep, healing, and regeneration
    - Theta (4-8 Hz): Creativity, intuition, and memory processing
    - Alpha (8-12 Hz): Relaxed alertness and mental clarity
    - Beta (12-30 Hz): Active thinking and problem-solving
    - Gamma (30-100 Hz): High-level cognitive functions and heightened perception
- Creativity and Innovation:
    - Alpha and Theta waves play crucial roles in fostering creativity.
    - Activities promoting these waves (e.g., showering, light meditation) can lead to creative insights.
    - Relaxed, less structured environments may be more conducive to innovative thinking than intense brainstorming sessions

- Analytical Thinking and Focus:
    - Beta waves are essential for tasks requiring concentration and logical reasoning.
    - These waves support the cognitive demands of data analysis and complex problem-solving in consulting.
- Stress Response and Cortical Inhibition:
    - Under stress, the limbic system can inhibit the prefrontal cortex, impairing higher-order thinking.
    - While evolutionarily beneficial, this "fight-or-flight" response can be counterproductive in modern professional settings.
- Mindful Breathing and Stress Management:
    - Mindful breathing techniques can counteract the stress response by activating the parasympathetic nervous system.
    - This practice promotes coherence between the brain, heart, and body, restoring optimal brain function.

Understanding these physiological processes underscores the importance of mindfulness practices in professional settings. By cultivating awareness of our brainwave states and learning to modulate them through mindfulness techniques, we can:

- Enhance our creative problem-solving abilities
- Improve focus and analytical thinking when needed

- Better manage stress responses in high-pressure situations

As we move forward, consider how you might integrate this knowledge into your daily work routine. Whether taking mindful breaks to access alpha and theta states for creativity or using breathing techniques to counteract stress responses, these practices can significantly enhance your professional performance and well-being.

Remember, the goal is not to eliminate stress entirely but to develop the ability to respond rather than react, maintaining cognitive clarity even in challenging situations. By mastering these mindfulness techniques, you're not just improving your work performance but cultivating a more balanced, resilient, and effective professional self.

Chapter 4: Mindful Breathing Techniques

*Feelings come and go like clouds in a windy sky.
Conscious breathing is my anchor.*

— Thích Nhất Hạnh

Imagine this: you're navigating a whirlwind of deadlines, meetings, and high-stakes decisions. Maybe you're clinching that make-or-break deal, saving a life in the ER, or untangling a stubborn knot of code. What if I told you that you could bring clarity and calm to those moments with just a few intentional breaths? Mastering mindful breathing techniques is like having a secret weapon, a tool that lets you pause and reset without missing a beat. It's a bit like taking a mini-vacation at your desk — no need for sunscreen, no overpriced drinks, just you and the power of your breath.

In this chapter, we'll dive into a range of breathing exercises designed to ground you in fundamental mindfulness. From diaphragmatic breathing, which invites deep, belly-filling breaths, to box breathing, a technique soldiers use to find calm amid chaos, you'll discover ways to enhance relaxation, lung function, and mental clarity. You'll even learn how something as simple as exhaling for a count of eight can be a natural tranquilliser. Each technique we explore will give you the tools to boost focus, control emotions, and build resilience — turning stressful moments into manageable, maybe even enjoyable, ones.

Basic Breathing Exercises: Your Lifeline in Chaos

Let's face it, high-pressure environments often feel like you're swimming against the tide. Whether you're a management consultant in a fast-paced meeting or a surgeon under the intense focus of an operating room, breathing can become your lifeline. The beauty of mindful breathing is its simplicity. No equipment, no special setting — you can do it anywhere, anytime.

Before jumping into specific techniques, here's a useful insight to remember rhythm is key to effective meditative breathing. Studies have shown that maintaining a steady, rhythmic pattern during breathing activates the parasympathetic nervous system, which is responsible for relaxation. The vagus nerve, a central component of this system, slows the heart rate and promotes calm. According to Jerath et al., slow, deep breathing activates this nerve, creating a state of physiological coherence, where the heart, brain, and body synchronise. This helps reduce stress and improve emotional regulation and decision-making.

The idea here is simple: rhythmic breathing = physiological balance. But here's the kicker — there's no need to exaggerate your breaths. The trick is to breathe naturally without forcing it. Let's dive into the techniques that will help you master this.

Diaphragmatic Breathing: Deep Belly Breaths

Diaphragmatic Breathing (also known as Deep Belly Breathing) is a breathing technique that encourages deep, full breaths by engaging the diaphragm. Unlike shallow chest breathing, which is common when stressed, diaphragmatic breathing allows for more oxygen intake and promotes relaxation. To practice, you breathe deeply into your abdomen, allowing it to expand like a balloon as you inhale, and then slowly exhale while contracting the abdominal muscles. This method is highly effective for reducing stress, lowering heart rate, and improving lung function, making it an excellent tool for relaxation and overall well-being:

1. Find a Comfortable Position:

- Sit or lie down in a comfortable position. Lying down flat or sitting upright in a chair is ideal.
- Place one hand on your chest and the other hand on your abdomen, just below your ribcage. This will help you feel the movement of your diaphragm as you breathe.

2. Relax Your Body:

- Close your eyes if it helps you focus and relax. If you prefer to keep your eyes open, find a focal point, such as a point on a roof or wall.
- Relax your shoulders, neck, and jaw. Release any tension in your body before you begin.

3. Inhale Deeply:
    - Breathe in slowly through your nose for a count of 4-6 seconds.
    - Focus on directing the air deep into your belly. You should feel your abdomen expand while keeping your chest relatively still. Your hand on your abdomen should rise while the one on your chest stays stable or moves only slightly.
    - Avoid forcing your breath; let it be smooth and natural.

4. Pause Briefly:
    - Once you've fully inhaled, pause for a brief moment (1-2 seconds), allowing your body to absorb the oxygen.

5. Exhale Slowly:
    - Purse your lips as if you are about to whistle, then exhale slowly through your mouth. Aim to exhale for a count of 6-8 seconds.

- As you exhale, contract your abdominal muscles slightly to push the air out from the diaphragm. Focus on slowly emptying your lungs.
- Feel your abdomen fall as you exhale, and ensure your chest remains relatively still.

6. Continue to Breathe Deeply:

- Repeat the cycle of inhalation and exhalation for 5 to 10 minutes. Maintain a steady rhythm throughout, with each inhale and exhale being slow and controlled.
- Focus on the sensations of the breath and the rise and fall of your abdomen, allowing your mind to relax.

7. Practice Regularly:

- Aim to practice diaphragmatic breathing daily, starting with 5 minutes and gradually extending to 10 minutes as you become more comfortable.
- With practice, you will become more aware of how shallow chest breathing feels compared to deep belly breathing, allowing you to shift to diaphragmatic breathing more naturally throughout the day.

Benefits of Regular Practice:

- Triggers the Relaxation Response: Engaging the parasympathetic nervous system helps reduce stress and anxiety.

- Increases Oxygen Intake: Enhances lung capacity and efficiency, leading to better oxygen delivery to your body.
- Promotes Mental Calmness: Helps improve focus and overall emotional regulation by bringing your attention to the present.

Box Breathing:

Box Breathing is a simple and effective technique for managing stress and promoting focus. It involves inhaling, holding the breath, exhaling, and holding again — each for an equal count, typically four seconds. This technique helps regulate your breath, calm the nervous system, and bring a sense of balance. It is widely used in high-stress environments, such as by soldiers, police and athletes, to improve concentration and emotional control. By practicing box breathing, you can quickly reduce anxiety, improve mental clarity, and enhance overall relaxation.

Here's how to get started with box breathing:

1. Find a Quiet Space:

- Sit comfortably with your back straight and feet flat on the floor. Rest your hands on your lap or by your sides.
- You can close your eyes to minimise distractions, but if you prefer to keep them open, focus on a single spot in your surroundings to help maintain concentration.

2. Inhale (4 Seconds):

- Breathe in slowly through your nose for a count of four. Focus on filling your lungs fully with air, expanding your abdomen as you inhale.
- Keep the breath smooth and controlled without forcing it.

3. Hold (4 Seconds):

- Once you've inhaled, hold your breath for another count of four. This pause helps regulate your breathing and gives the body time to absorb oxygen.
- During this hold, stay relaxed and avoid tensing your body.

4. Exhale (4 Seconds):

- Exhale slowly and smoothly through your mouth for a count of four. Focus on expelling all the air from your lungs, letting your abdomen fall as you release the breath.
- Keep the exhale controlled without rushing or pushing.

5. Hold (4 Seconds):

- After exhaling, hold your breath again for another count of four. This final pause completes the cycle before you start the next breath.

6. Repeat the Cycle:

- Continue the box breathing cycle for at least three repetitions, or ideally for 4 minutes. Adjust the duration based on your comfort, starting with shorter counts if needed (e.g., three seconds) and gradually increasing to four seconds as you become more comfortable.

Benefits of Regular Practice:

- Reduces Stress and Anxiety: Box breathing activates the parasympathetic nervous system, which lowers heart rate and reduces the body's fight-or-flight response, promoting relaxation and calmness.
- Improves Focus and Clarity: Regular practice helps you clear your mind and enhances concentration, making it useful for stressful situations or when you need to perform under pressure.
- Enhances Emotional Regulation: By controlling your breath and maintaining a steady rhythm, you gain greater emotional stability, which can help you manage anxiety, anger, or frustration more effectively.
- Balances the Autonomic Nervous System: Box breathing helps balance the sympathetic (fight or flight) and parasympathetic (rest-and-digest) nervous systems, improving overall health and reducing stress levels.

- Increases Lung Capacity: Slow, deep breathing increases lung efficiency and improves overall respiratory health over time.

4-7-8 Breathing:

Popularised by Dr. Andrew Weil, 4-7-8 Breathing is a powerful relaxation technique that uses a specific breath pattern to help calm the mind and body. The method involves inhaling for 4 counts, holding the breath for 7 counts, and exhaling for 8 counts. This extended exhalation phase activates the parasympathetic nervous system, reducing stress and promoting a deep sense of calm. Regular practice of 4-7-8 breathing can improve sleep, lower anxiety, and enhance overall emotional balance, making it an effective tool for immediate relaxation and long-term mental well-being.

To perform the 4-7-8 technique, follow these steps:

1. Position Yourself:

- Sit comfortably with your back straight, or if you prefer, lie down in a relaxed position. Ensure your spine is aligned, allowing optimal airflow during the exercise.

2. Place Your Tongue:

- Rest the tip of your tongue against the ridge of tissue just behind your upper front teeth. Keep your tongue in this position throughout the entire breathing exercise. This helps maintain a smooth flow during exhalation.

3. Exhale Completely:

   - Begin by exhaling fully through your mouth, making a soft "whoosh" sound as you gently push all the air out of your lungs. This initial exhale clears out stale air and prepares your lungs for deeper inhalation.

4. Inhale Quietly (Count of 4):

   - Close your mouth and inhale slowly and quietly through your nose for a count of four. Focus on drawing the air deeply into your lungs, allowing your abdomen to expand as you breathe in.

5. Hold Your Breath (Count of 7):

   - Hold your breath for a count of seven. This pause allows the oxygen to circulate more effectively through your bloodstream, promoting relaxation and a calming effect on your nervous system.

6. Exhale Completely (Count of 8):

   - Exhale completely through your mouth, making a "whoosh" sound for a count of eight. Focus on pushing all the air out of your lungs. This longer exhale helps empty the lungs fully and enhances the relaxation response.

7. Repeat the Cycle:

- Initially, repeat the cycle up to four times. As you become more comfortable with the technique, you can gradually work up to eight cycles. Avoid exceeding eight cycles per session, especially when starting.

Benefits of Regular Practice:

- Reduces Stress and Anxiety: The 4-7-8 technique helps activate the parasympathetic nervous system, which counteracts the stress response. By focusing on controlled breathing, this technique lowers heart rate and reduces anxiety, promoting a sense of calm.
- Improves Sleep Quality: Slowing down your breath and extending the exhale helps calm the mind, making it an effective tool for improving sleep and combating insomnia.
- Enhances Lung Function: Practicing deep, controlled breathing increases lung capacity and efficiency, gradually strengthening the respiratory system and improving oxygen exchange.
- Regulates the Nervous System: The controlled breath pattern slows down the autonomic nervous system, helping regulate both the sympathetic and parasympathetic systems.
- Promotes Mindfulness: Focusing on breath counts creates a meditative effect, anchoring your attention to the present moment and reducing mental clutter.

Mindful Breathing Awareness:

Mindful Breathing Awareness is a simple yet effective practice that brings your attention to the natural rhythm of your breath, fostering presence and awareness. By focusing on the sensations of breathing — such as the feeling of air entering your nostrils, filling your lungs, and leaving your body — you anchor your mind in the present moment. This practice helps reduce stress, enhance focus, and improve emotional regulation. It's particularly useful in promoting relaxation and building mental clarity, making it an accessible tool for cultivating mindfulness and improving overall well-being. This technique doesn't just help with mindfulness; it also serves as an anchor, bringing your attention back to the present moment whenever your mind wanders.

To practice mindful breathing awareness, consider the following:

1. Focus on Your Breath:

- Sit or lie down in a comfortable position, ensuring your body is relaxed and supported. You can close your eyes to reduce distractions, helping you concentrate more deeply on your breath.
- Begin by simply bringing your attention to your breathing, allowing yourself to settle into the natural rhythm of your breath without trying to change or control it.

2. Observe Sensations:

- Pay close attention to the physical sensations that arise as you breathe. Notice the coolness of the air as it enters your nostrils, how your lungs gently expand, and the feeling of the breath leaving your body. Focus on how your abdomen rises and falls with each breath.
- Be fully present with each inhale and exhale, observing the flow of air through your body and how it feels in the moment.

3. Use a Calming Focus:

- To enhance your practice, silently repeat a calming word or phrase with each breath, such as "peace" or "calm." You can say the word in your mind as you inhale and exhale, using it as an anchor to deepen your focus.
- This simple phrase can serve as a reminder to relax and stay centred, helping reinforce a state of mental calm and emotional balance.

4. Gentle Persistence:

- When your mind inevitably wanders, gently redirect your attention back to your breath without self-judgment. It's natural for your mind to drift; this practice is about acknowledging that and gently returning your focus to the present moment.

- Each time you bring your awareness back to your breath, you strengthen your focus and improve your mental discipline. Over time, this will help improve your overall mindfulness and concentration.

Benefits of Regular Practice:

- Reduces Stress and Anxiety: Mindful breathing activates the parasympathetic nervous system, promoting relaxation and reducing stress hormones like cortisol. Focusing on the breath creates a buffer between yourself and stressful thoughts, allowing for emotional regulation.
- Improves Focus and Attention: Regular mindful breathing strengthens the mind's ability to concentrate. Each time you bring your attention back to the breath, you reinforce neural pathways that support attention control, enhancing your ability to focus during daily tasks.
- Promotes Emotional Awareness: By observing the sensations of your breath, you become more in tune with your body and emotions. This helps cultivate greater self-awareness and emotional resilience, allowing you to respond to situations more thoughtfully rather than reactively.
- Enhances Overall Well-being: Mindful breathing improves your connection to the present moment, reducing ruminative thinking and promoting a sense

of peace. This simple practice can be incorporated into daily life, bringing a sense of calm and clarity to your routine.

- By regularly practising mindful breathing awareness, you will develop a deeper sense of relaxation, focus, and emotional balance. Over time, this practice can lead to a greater sense of well-being and improved mental clarity. Incorporating mindful breathing into your routine creates space to pause and reset, enhancing your ability to remain calm and focused during high-stress situations.

Vagal Breathing Technique:

Vagal Breathing Technique is a focused breathing method designed to activate the vagus nerve, which plays a key role in regulating the body's parasympathetic nervous system. By extending the exhalation phase, this technique helps calm the nervous system, reduce stress, and promote relaxation. This longer exhalation stimulates the vagus nerve, lowering heart rate and fostering a deep sense of calm, making it an effective tool for managing anxiety and improving focus.

Research by De Couck et al. has indicated that vagal breathing, which emphasises longer exhalations, can significantly improve decision-making tasks. Here's a breakdown of this technique:

1. Inhale Deeply (Count of 4):

- Breathe in deeply through your nose for a count of four. Focus on filling your lungs completely, expanding your abdomen as you draw in the air. This deep inhalation helps to oxygenate your body and primes your system for relaxation.

2. Exhale Slowly (Count of 6-8):

- Exhale slowly and completely through your mouth for a count of six or eight. The key here is to make the exhalation longer than the inhalation, as this activates the vagus nerve and promotes relaxation. You should feel your abdomen contract as you expel the air, helping your body release tension.

3. Focus on Longer Exhalations:

- Throughout the practice, maintain your focus on making each exhale longer than the inhale. This intentional lengthening of the exhalation stimulates the parasympathetic nervous system via the vagus nerve, enhancing your body's ability to stay calm and focused.

4. Repeat the Cycle:

- Continue this breathing cycle for two to three minutes before engaging in tasks that require decision-making or cognitive effort. This practice helps to calm the nervous system and prepare your brain for higher-order thinking, improving cognitive performance and decision-making abilities.

Benefits of Regular Practice:

- Improved Decision-Making: Research by De Couck et al. indicates that vagal breathing significantly enhances cognitive function and decision-making tasks, particularly when exhalations are longer than inhalations. This occurs because longer exhalations activate the parasympathetic nervous system, which fosters better focus and mental clarity.

- Stress Reduction: Vagal breathing helps to reduce stress by lowering heart rate and promoting relaxation through the vagus nerve, which is responsible for calming the body's fight-or-flight response.

- Enhanced Emotional Regulation: Regular practice of this technique improves your ability to manage emotions by keeping your nervous system in a balanced state, which is essential during decision-making and high-pressure tasks.

- Increased Focus and Calm: By practising before cognitive tasks, you enter a calm, focused state, helping you make clearer, more thoughtful decisions rather than impulsive ones driven by stress or anxiety.

Incorporating vagal breathing into your routine for just a few minutes before challenging mental tasks can lead to improved cognitive performance, better decision-making, and a more relaxed, focused mindset. These breathing exercises can create a foundation for better decision-making by promoting a calmer and more focused mind. Whether you're a management consultant facing intense deadlines or a healthcare professional navigating high-stakes situations, mastering breath control can become a vital tool in your arsenal, helping you make wiser, more deliberate choices.

Practical Integration:

Incorporating mindful breathing techniques into your daily routine can profoundly impact your mental clarity, emotional stability, and overall well-being. Think of it as weaving moments of calm into the fabric of your day — small but powerful adjustments that bring significant benefits over time. Whether you're starting your morning, calming pre-meeting nerves, or winding down after a long day, these techniques offer simple, effective ways to manage stress and enhance focus.

Introducing Breathing Practices into Daily Life

To begin, try integrating diaphragmatic breathing into your routine. A short session first thing in the morning or before bed can set a peaceful tone for the day or help you unwind before sleep. Start with a few minutes, focusing on deep belly breaths, and you'll likely notice the calming effects immediately.

When facing stressful moments like a big meeting or high-pressure decision, box breathing can be an excellent tool for regaining focus and composure. A few rounds of this structured breathing exercise can calm your nerves and sharpen your attention, making you feel more in control. And if you're looking to fully relax after a particularly intense day, the 4-7-8 breathing technique can work wonders by helping you transition from a busy mind to a calm, restful state.

As you become more accustomed to these practices, you'll start to see a shift in how you handle stress and approach daily challenges. Whether you're negotiating deals, performing complex tasks, or managing pressing deadlines, mindful breathing will help you stay grounded, focused, and effective.

Key Takeaways

Over the course of this chapter, we've explored various mindful breathing techniques designed to enhance focus, reduce stress, and improve overall well-being in high-pressure professional environments. Let's recap the key insights:

- Basic Breathing Exercises:
    - Diaphragmatic Breathing: Encourages deep belly breaths for increased oxygen flow and relaxation
    - Box Breathing: A structured technique for resetting breath and calming mind and body

- 4-7-8 Breathing: Acts as a natural tranquilizer for the nervous system
- Mindful Breathing Awareness: Focuses on being present with each breath
- Vagal Breathing: Emphasizes longer exhalations to improve decision-making
- Key Benefits:
  - Reduces stress and anxiety
  - Improves focus and mental clarity
  - Enhances emotional regulation
  - Boosts cognitive performance
  - Promotes better sleep quality
- Practical Integration:
  - Start with short sessions and gradually increase duration
  - Use different techniques for specific situations (e.g., box breathing before meetings)
  - Incorporate breathing exercises into daily routines (morning, before bed, during breaks)
- Remember:
  - Consistency is key: Regular practice yields the most significant benefits
  - No special equipment needed: These techniques can be practiced anywhere, anytime
  - Personalize your approach: Experiment with different techniques to find what works best for you

By integrating these mindful breathing practices into your daily life, you're equipping yourself with powerful tools to navigate the challenges of high-pressure professional environments. These techniques offer a way to reset, refocus, and respond to stress with greater calm and clarity.

As you move forward, consider how you can incorporate these breathing exercises into your routine. Whether it's taking a few deep breaths before an important meeting or practicing box breathing during your commute, each mindful breath is a step towards greater resilience and effectiveness in your professional life.

Chapter 5: Advanced Techniques for Deep Relaxation

> *Calm mind brings inner strength and self-confidence, so that's very important for good health.*
>
> — Dalai Lama

Once you've mastered basic breathing techniques, you might want to explore more advanced methods that foster deeper relaxation. These techniques are designed to reduce your stress levels and help you achieve a calm focus, which can be especially helpful in high-pressure situations.

Progressive Muscle Relaxation (PMR) with Breath

Progressive Muscle Relaxation with Breath is a technique that combines controlled breathing with the gradual tensing and releasing of muscle groups throughout the body. This practice encourages deep relaxation by synchronising breath with muscle contraction and release, helping to relieve tension and promote a sense of calm. As you inhale, you tense a specific muscle group; as you exhale, you release that tension, allowing stress to flow out of your body. This method is especially useful for reducing physical stress, calming the mind, and grounding yourself in the present moment, making it an ideal tool for managing anxiety and promoting relaxation. To enhance the experience, you can listen to a PMR audio meditation for guided support.

1. Get Into a Comfortable Position:

- Lie Down or Sit Comfortably: Choose a position that allows your body to fully relax. Lying down on a mat or bed is ideal, but you can also sit in a comfortable chair with your feet flat on the ground and your hands resting on your lap.
- Close Your Eyes: Closing your eyes helps minimise distractions, allowing you to focus on your breath and muscle sensations.

2. Deep Breathing to Centre Yourself:

- Inhale Slowly: Take a deep breath through your nose for a count of four. Feel your abdomen expand as you inhale.
- Exhale Slowly: Release the breath slowly through your mouth for a count of six or eight. This helps calm your nervous system and prepares your body for relaxation.
- Repeat 2-3 Times: Take a few deep breaths before you begin the muscle relaxation sequence to settle into the exercise.

3. Tense and Relax Your Muscles:

- Start with Your Feet: Focus on your feet. Inhale deeply, and as you do, tense the muscles in your feet — curl your toes or flex your feet.
- Hold the Tension: Hold the tension for about 5 seconds, feeling the tightness in your muscles.
- Release as You Exhale: Exhale slowly through your mouth while releasing the tension in your feet. Imagine the stress flowing out with your breath and feel the muscles relax completely.
- Move Up Through Your Body: After your feet, move your attention to your legs, thighs, abdomen, arms, hands, shoulders, neck, and finally your face. For each muscle group, inhale as you tense, hold for a few seconds, and exhale as you relax.

4. Synchronise Breathing with Muscle Relaxation:

- For each muscle group, inhale deeply while tensing the muscles, then exhale slowly while relaxing the muscles. This synchronisation allows for deeper relaxation and a stronger mind-body connection.
- Visualise the tension leaving your body with each exhale and focus on the sensation of relaxation spreading through the muscles.

5. Focus on Areas of Tension:

- If you notice tension in certain muscle groups, such as your shoulders or neck, focus more on those areas.

Inhale, tense those muscles slightly more than others, and visualise the tension melting away on the exhale.

- If needed, repeat the tensing and relaxing process for these areas to ensure full relaxation.

6. End with Full-Body Relaxation:

- Take a few deep breaths while focusing on your whole body being relaxed. Imagine any remaining tension dissolving with each exhale.
- You can stay in this relaxed state for as long as you like, simply breathing deeply and enjoying the calm feeling.

7. Enhance the Experience with Guided Audio:

- Use a pre-recorded Progressive Muscle Relaxation (PMR) audio meditation for additional guidance. These audios can walk you through each muscle group and help maintain your focus during the exercise.
- Listening to soothing music or a guided voice can deepen relaxation by creating a calming atmosphere.

Benefits of Regular Practice:

- Reduces Physical Tension: PMR helps release muscle tightness and tension that can accumulate due to stress or anxiety.

- Calms the Nervous System: Deep breathing and muscle relaxation activate the parasympathetic nervous system, promoting a calm and restful state.
- Improves Sleep Quality: Practicing PMR before bed can help release physical and mental stress, improving sleep quality.
- Increases Body Awareness: Focusing on different muscle groups makes you more aware of where you hold tension, helping you manage stress more effectively in daily life.
- Regularly practising Progressive Muscle Relaxation with Breath will help you experience a deeper sense of relaxation, improve stress management, and enhance overall well-being.

Alternate Nostril Breathing ((Nadi Shodhana)

Alternate Nostril Breathing is a calming yogic technique that balances the flow of breath through both nostrils, promoting mental clarity and emotional equilibrium. Altering the nostrils during inhalation and exhalation helps synchronise the left and right hemispheres of the brain, creating a sense of balance and focus. This method is particularly effective for reducing stress, enhancing concentration, and fostering a state of calm. It's a simple yet powerful tool to incorporate into daily mindfulness or meditation practices, supporting physical relaxation and mental clarity.

1. Find a Comfortable Position:

- Sit Comfortably: Choose a seated position with a straight spine, either cross-legged on the floor or sitting in a chair with your feet flat on the ground. Rest your hands on your knees or in your lap.
- Close Your Eyes: Closing your eyes helps eliminate distractions and encourages inward focus. Focus on your breath and relax your body before beginning the technique.

2. Start the Breathing Cycle:

- Position Your Hand: Lift your right hand and use your thumb to gently block your right nostril. Place your ring finger near your left nostril, but leave it open for now.
- Inhale Through the Left Nostril: With the right nostril closed, inhale deeply through your left nostril, filling your lungs completely. Focus on a slow, smooth breath.
- Switch Sides: After inhaling, use your ring finger to close your left nostril, then release your right nostril and exhale fully through the right nostril.
- Continue the Pattern: Now, inhale through your right nostril (with the left nostril closed), then switch again by closing the right nostril and exhaling through the left nostril. This completes one full cycle of alternate nostril breathing.

3. Focus on Balanced Breathing:

- Maintain Even Breaths: As you alternate between nostrils, ensure that each inhale and exhale is smooth and of equal length. This helps harmonise the body's energy and promotes balance.
- Concentration on the Breath: Throughout the practice, keep your focus entirely on your breath. Feel the flow of air entering and exiting your body and allow distracting thoughts to fade as you return your attention to the rhythm of your breath.

4. Repeat the Cycle:

- 10 Rounds or More: Continue inhaling through one nostril and exhaling through the other for 10 rounds or as long as you feel comfortable. Each round consists of one complete inhale and exhale through alternating nostrils.
- Deepen the Practice: As you become more comfortable, you can extend the practice to 15 or 20 rounds, focusing on deepening each breath to maximise the calming effect.

Enhance the Experience:

- Set an Intention: Before starting, set an intention for your practice. This could be to reduce stress, improve focus, or simply achieve a sense of balance.

- Use a Peaceful Space: Practicing in a quiet, peaceful environment can enhance the calming effects of this technique. Dim lighting or soft music can help you relax more deeply.

Benefits of Regular Practice:

- Balances Brain Hemispheres: Alternate nostril breathing harmonises the brain's two hemispheres, improving mental clarity and overall cognitive function.
- Reduces Stress and Anxiety: By calming the nervous system and regulating the breath, this technique effectively reduces stress, anxiety, and mental tension.
- Improves Concentration: The rhythmic, balanced breathing helps clear mental fog and improve focus, making it a great tool before tasks requiring mental clarity.
- Enhances Emotional Balance: Alternate nostril breathing fosters emotional stability by balancing the breath and mind, helping you feel more grounded and centred.

Regular practice of Alternate Nostril Breathing helps achieve emotional calm, improved concentration, and overall mental clarity. With just 10 rounds, you can experience a significant reduction in stress and a greater sense of balance.

Guided Visualization with Breath

Pairing Breathing with Visualisation is a simple yet highly effective technique for promoting relaxation and cultivating positivity. This method combines controlled breathing with mental imagery, allowing you to visualise yourself in a peaceful, serene setting while focusing on slow, deep breaths. As you inhale, you imagine drawing in calmness and peace; exhaling, you release tension and negative thoughts. Combining breath and visualisation helps anchor the mind, reducing stress and creating emotional balance and well-being. It's an accessible tool for enhancing mindfulness and deep relaxation.

1. Find a Comfortable Position:

- Sit or Lie Down Comfortably: Choose a position where your body is supported and at ease. You can sit cross-legged, in a chair with your feet flat on the floor or lie down on your back.
- Close Your Eyes: Closing your eyes will help you focus on your inner world and fully immerse in the visualisation.

2. Begin Deep Breathing:

- Inhale Deeply: Breathe slowly through your nose, allowing your abdomen to expand as you fill your lungs with air.

- Exhale Slowly: Release the breath through your mouth, feeling your body relax as you release any tension.
- Repeat 2-3 Times: Take a few deep breaths to ground yourself before moving into the visualisation process.

3. Choose Your Visualisation:

- Pick a Serene Setting: Visualise a peaceful place that brings you a sense of calm, such as a beach, a forest, a mountaintop, or any other location where you feel at ease.
- Engage Your Senses: As you picture this place, engage all your senses. Imagine the colours around you, the sounds of nature (like birds, waves, or wind), the texture of the ground, and the smell of the air. This immersive sensory experience deepens the calming effect.
- Focus on Details: The more vivid and detailed your visualisation, the more effectively it will calm your mind and promote relaxation.

4. Pair Visualisation with Breathing:

- Inhale Calm and Peace: As you take each slow, deep breath, visualise drawing in calm, peace, and positive energy from your serene environment. Feel the tranquillity of the scene entering your body.

- Exhale Tension and Negativity: As you exhale, imagine releasing all tension, stress, and negative thoughts. Picture them leaving your body and dissolving into the air, far away from your calm setting.
- Continue the Cycle: With each inhale, invite more peace into your body, and with each exhale, let go of more tension and negativity. Repeat this pattern for several minutes, fully immersing yourself in the experience.

5. Deepen the Visualisation:

- Focus on Emotions: As you continue, focus on the emotional state this visualisation brings. Does it make you feel safe, content, or free? Allow those feelings to grow stronger with each breath.
- Stay Present in the Scene: Keep your mind fully engaged with the scene you've created, continuing to explore its beauty and peacefulness. This deeper connection enhances relaxation and fosters a sense of well-being.

6. End the Practice Gradually:

- Return Slowly: When you're ready to finish, gently bring your awareness back to the present moment while keeping the calm feelings you've cultivated. You can stretch or take a few more deep breaths before opening your eyes.

- Reflect on the Experience: Take a moment to notice how you feel after the practice, acknowledging the relaxation and mental clarity you've achieved.

Benefits of Regular Practice:

- Promotes Deep Relaxation: Combining deep breathing with calming visualisation relaxes the body and mind, reducing tension and promoting inner peace.
- Enhances Positivity: Visualisation helps shift your focus from stress to a positive, calming image, cultivating a sense of well-being and emotional stability.
- Reduces Stress and Anxiety: This technique helps regulate the nervous system by focusing on peaceful imagery and synchronised breathing, reducing the effects of stress and anxiety.
- Boosts Mental Clarity and Focus: Combining breathing and visualisation helps clear mental clutter, making it easier to focus and think clearly.
- Regularly practicing Breathing with Visualisation can achieve a profound sense of relaxation and positivity, making it a valuable tool for reducing stress and enhancing emotional well-being.

Integrating Breathing into Your Daily Routine

Incorporating mindful breathing into your day doesn't require a major lifestyle change. These "breath breaks" can be woven into transitions between tasks, during meetings, or even while commuting. Let's explore how to integrate these techniques seamlessly into your routine.

Breath Breaks During Transitions

Moving from one task to another without pause can allow stress to build up over time. By inserting mindful breath breaks between activities, you can reset your mental state and prevent stress from accumulating. For example, after finishing a meeting, take a minute to practice diaphragmatic breathing or box breathing before diving into your next project. This brief intermission can ground you, providing clarity and reducing stress so you can approach your next task with renewed focus.

Mindful Breathing During Meetings

Meetings often test your ability to juggle thoughts, ideas, and responses. To maintain focus and calm, try a quick breathing exercise before speaking or making an important point. Inhale deeply, hold for a moment and exhale slowly. This will calm your nerves and help you collect your thoughts, ensuring a more thoughtful response. Practising mindful breathing during meetings lets you stay fully present, engaged, and composed.

Breathing While Commuting

Whether on the train, bus or even walking, commuting offers a great opportunity to practice mindful breathing. Instead of letting your mind wander or focusing on the day's stresses, use this time to centre yourself with rhythmic breathing. A simple, coherent breathing technique — inhaling and exhaling for an equal number of counts — can help reduce anxiety and prepare you for the day ahead. Even short intervals of mindful breathing during your commute can significantly improve your mental state over time.

Setting Reminders for Breathing

In our fast-paced world, it's easy to forget to take a moment for mindful breathing. Set gentle reminders on your phone or computer to pause for a quick breathing exercise throughout the day. There are apps available that guide you through short, focused breathing sessions, making it easier to incorporate into your routine. Treat these reminders as non-negotiable — like an important meeting — and soon, mindful breathing will become a natural part of your day.

The Impact of Breath Control on Decision-Making

The power of mindful breathing goes beyond relaxation — it can directly influence how you make decisions, particularly in high-pressure environments. When you're stressed, your breathing becomes shallow and rapid, which signals your brain that you're in distress. However, intentionally slowing your breath can calm your nervous system and maintain emotional balance, which is crucial for clear-headed decision-making.

Breath control helps manage emotions, reduces anxiety, and allows you to approach challenges with a calm, focused mindset. Studies by Zaccaro et al have shown that slow, deep breathing can enhance mental clarity, vigour, and alertness while reducing confusion and anxiety. Maintaining this emotional equilibrium allows you to make more rational decisions, even under pressure.

Neuroscience research further reveals how breath control affects brain activity. Techniques like Pranayama have been shown to increase alpha brain waves — associated with relaxed focus — and decrease beta waves, which are linked to mental chatter. Functional MRI (fMRI) studies also show increased activity in the prefrontal cortex during mindful breathing, a region crucial for emotional regulation and decision-making. By harnessing the power of mindful breathing, you can improve your cognitive capabilities and make better decisions, even in the most demanding situations.

Key Takeaways

This chapter has explored several advanced techniques for achieving deep relaxation and enhancing mindfulness in professional settings. Let's recap the key insights:

- Advanced Relaxation Techniques:

- - o Progressive Muscle Relaxation (PMR) with Breath: Combines controlled breathing with muscle tension and release
  - o Alternate Nostril Breathing: Balances breath flow and promotes mental clarity
  - o Guided Visualisation with Breath: Pairs controlled breathing with calming mental imagery
- Key Benefits:
  - o Reduces physical and mental tension
  - o Balances brain hemispheres and improves cognitive function
  - o Enhances emotional regulation and promotes positivity
  - o Activates the parasympathetic nervous system for stress relief
  - o Improves sleep quality and overall well-being
- Integrating Breathing into Daily Routine:
  - o Take breath breaks during transitions between tasks
  - o Practice mindful breathing during meetings
  - o Utilise commute time for breathing exercises
  - o Set reminders for regular breathing practice
- Impact on Decision-Making:
  - o Controlled breathing enhances mental clarity and focus

- o Reduces anxiety and promotes emotional balance
- o Improves cognitive capabilities in high-pressure situations
- Remember:
    - o Consistency is key: Regular practice yields the most significant benefits
    - o Personalise your approach: Experiment with different techniques to find what works best for you
    - o Start small: Begin with short sessions and gradually increase the duration
    - o Use in high-stress moments: These techniques can provide immediate relief when needed

By incorporating these advanced relaxation techniques into your professional life, you're equipping yourself with powerful tools to manage stress, enhance focus, and improve decision-making. These practices benefit your immediate well-being and contribute to long-term resilience and effectiveness in high-pressure environments.

Whether starting your day with Progressive Muscle Relaxation, using Alternate Nostril Breathing before an important meeting, or practising Extended Exhalation during your commute, each mindful moment contributes to your overall performance and well-being. With consistent practice, you'll likely notice a significant improvement in your ability to stay calm, focused, and effective, even in the most challenging professional situations.

Chapter 6: Mindfulness Meditation Practices

The bird flies through the sky and leaves no trace

— *Zen proverb*

Mindfulness meditation is like giving your brain a spa day, minus the hassle of traffic or the distraction of whale music. For high-performing professionals juggling endless responsibilities, finding that elusive "me-time" can feel impossible. That's where mindfulness meditation comes in — a collection of techniques designed to fit seamlessly into your busy life. Imagine hitting the reset button on your stress levels while waiting for your coffee to brew. That's the power of mindfulness meditation, and in this chapter, we'll explore how these practices can inject calm and clarity into your hectic schedule.

We'll cover various meditation techniques, from guided meditations that walk you through each step like a personal coach to silent sessions where you are the boss of your zen. You'll also learn how setting intentions can supercharge your practice and why shorter, frequent sessions may become your secret weapon against stress. So, get ready to unbuckle, relax, and dive into a journey of calm amidst the chaos.

Are Mindfulness and Meditation the Same?

Although mindfulness and meditation are often used together, they serve different purposes and can be practised separately.

Mindfulness is the practice of being fully present and engaged in the current moment, aware of where you are and what you're doing, without being overwhelmed or overly reactive. You can practice mindfulness anywhere, whether eating, walking, or even working. It's about being grounded in the here and now, paying attention to your thoughts, feelings, and surroundings without judgment.

Meditation is a more structured practice aimed at training the mind. It usually involves sitting quietly, focusing on a specific object (like the breath or a mantra), and letting go of distractions to cultivate a state of calm and concentration. There are many forms of meditation, such as focused attention meditation, loving-kindness meditation, and transcendental meditation.

Mindfulness meditation blends the two: during this practice, you focus on your breath or bodily sensations, observing them without judgment. This strengthens your ability to be mindful in everyday life, even when not meditating. In short, meditation is a tool to cultivate mindfulness, which can be practised both within and outside meditation.

Being Present vs. Being in the Present

A common question I get is: "Does being present mean you don't think about the past or future?" Not quite. While similar, there are subtle differences.

Being present means actively engaging with what you're doing now without distractions. It's about fully paying attention to your experience. Imagine you're in a meeting. Being present in a mindfulness way would mean noticing the tone of your colleagues' voices, being aware of your emotional reactions, and paying attention to your body language, all without judgment or distraction, just observing each moment as it is. If you're present, you're not thinking about your phone or what you will do later. It is about the quality of how you are experiencing the moment.

As an example, one of my favourite mindfulness activities is washing dishes. It's a simple task that allows me to focus on the warm water, the lather of soap, and the sound of placing dishes on the drying rack. It's not intellectually demanding, and I can drift into a peaceful, calm state while ticking a chore off the list.

On the other hand, being in the present generally refers to simply living in the current moment, but without the intentional focus that mindfulness brings. It can involve physically being there and somewhat aware of what's happening around you, but it may lack the deeper, conscious engagement. Looking at the previous example in a different way, being in the present could mean you are listening to what's being said and aware of the discussion, but you might also be distracted by thoughts of an upcoming task or replaying a past conversation in your mind. You're physically there but not fully anchored in the moment.

Mindfulness and Flow

The performance state of flow, often called "being in the zone," is a mental state where a person becomes fully immersed and focused on a task, experiencing high levels of concentration, enjoyment, and productivity. It was first described by psychologist Mihaly Csikszentmihalyi in his book *Flow: The Psychology of Optimal Experience*. In flow, time seems to either slow down or speed up, and external distractions fade away, allowing individuals to give their full attention to the activity.

Flow, or what's often called being "in the zone," is that state where you're completely absorbed in what you're doing, feeling a deep sense of focus and even enjoyment. It was first described by psychologist Mihaly Csikszentmihalyi in his book *Flow: The Psychology of Optimal Experience*, as a moment when time either seems to fly by or slow down, and you're so engaged that everything else fades into the background.

If you work in a high-performance job — like management consulting, for example — you've probably experienced flow.

Whether you're solving complex problems, delivering a critical presentation, or handling the fast pace of client demands, flow helps you stay focused and keep your momentum going. It's that feeling when you're so dialled in that distractions disappear, and you're working at your peak performance level.

Key characteristics of flow include:

- Intense focus and concentration – You are completely absorbed in the task.
- Clear goals and immediate feedback – You know exactly what to do and how well they do.
- A balance between skill and challenge – The task is challenging but achievable, matching your skill level.
- Loss of self-consciousness – You are so engaged that you're not preoccupied with self-doubt or external judgments.
- A sense of control – Despite the challenge, you feel in control of their actions.
- Intrinsic motivation – The task is rewarding, and you're driven by the joy of doing it rather than external rewards.

Mindfulness and flow share several key qualities, including focusing on the present moment, full immersion in the task at hand, and a heightened awareness. Both involve minimising distractions and deep thinking, allowing for focused concentration and engagement. Additionally, they are linked to enhanced well-being, as mindfulness promotes relaxation and clarity, while flow fosters a sense of fulfilment and intrinsic motivation. Both states also improve performance, reducing mental clutter and allowing you to function at your best.

Guided Meditations for Beginners

So, the question is what can you do to help develop the skills necessary to achieve these states of heightened awareness, being present and peak performance?

Personally, guided meditations are a great place to start if you're new to mindfulness, it's where I cut my teeth. Guided meditations provide structure and clarity, a calming voice walking you through the process. In a world where everything seems like a chore, guided meditation takes the pressure off by offering step-by-step guidance.

Free apps like Insight Timer offer thousands of meditations for various scenarios — whether you need a quick five-minute reset between meetings or something longer before bed. For a more personalised experience, premium subscriptions like Headspace or Calm provide curated content, track your progress, and even include sleep stories.

When I first started practising mindful meditation, I used guided tools to help me focus on the practice without worrying about technique. Here are some of my favourites:

- Guided mindfulness meditation by Jon Kabat-Zinn
- Guided meditation by Tara Brach
- Headspace (an app)

One tip to enhance your meditation experience is to set an intention. Think of it as setting your GPS before a journey — without a clear intention, meditation can feel aimless. For example, if you intend to focus on gratitude, your mind has a direction which brings more depth to your practice.

Before the session you can say to yourself, "During this session, I'll focus on appreciating the good in my life." Then, as you meditate, gently bring your awareness back to things you're thankful for whenever your mind wanders. It's a simple, intentional way to guide your meditation.

Also, short, frequent sessions are often more effective and easier to maintain than long, sporadic ones. Five or ten minutes here and there can make a big difference, and they fit into even the busiest schedules. A brief morning meditation can set the tone for the day, a midday pause can help you reset, and a short session before bed can help you wind down.

Silent Meditation Practices

For high-achieving professionals, silent meditation is an empowering practice. Without external guidance, you're free to explore your focus points — your breath, body sensations, or open awareness.

Imagine sitting quietly, focusing on the rhythm of your breath. As thoughts arise, you acknowledge them without judgement, if your mind wanders, then gently return to your breathing. This helps you develop a stronger connection to yourself and a heightened sense of present-moment awareness.

People often ask what "observe a thought" means without interacting. Here's a simple analogy: Imagine you're sitting by a river watching leaves float downstream. You can focus on each leaf, watching it from the moment you first see it to the moment it vanishes from your sight, chances are you will miss all the other leaves floating downstream. Otherwise, you can simply notice the leaf and acknowledge that it has passed and let it go. Now, imagine that each leaf carries a thought. Rather than analysing it or following where it might lead, you notice it and let it drift away and bring your attention back to your breathing. When your mind wanders again, with no judgement, do the same. Then rinse and repeat.

This practice helps you observe thoughts without getting caught up in them. As you strengthen this skill, staying present and maintaining calm becomes easier, even when your mind wants to wander.

Creating a peaceful environment can enhance your meditation practice. Find a quiet corner in your home, away from distractions, and personalise it with comfortable cushions or dim lighting. Creating a serene space makes it easier to settle into meditation and focus on your inner world.

For beginners, start with just five minutes of silent meditation daily and gradually extend the duration. This incremental approach builds stamina and makes the practice less daunting.

Practical Tips for Sustaining a Meditation Habit

Consistency is key when it comes to mindfulness meditation. Here are some practical tips to help you stay committed:

- Set a timer for your sessions. Knowing there's an endpoint makes the practice feel more manageable.
- Link meditation to an existing habit, like brushing your teeth in the morning or winding down before bed. This helps you integrate meditation seamlessly into your daily routine.
- Use reminders — whether an alarm on your phone or a post-it on your computer, a gentle nudge can prompt you to take that mindful pause.

The Purpose of Meditation: It's Not About Mastery

I often hear people say, "I don't meditate. I have tried but I'm no good at it." Meditation isn't something you need to master. In fact, trying to master it requires effort and doing, the opposite of the purpose of taking the time to meditate, which is just about being. It's about sitting in the moment and focusing on your breath, not achieving perfection. The true goal of meditation isn't to become a master meditator — it's to gain the tools to master life.

By embracing mindfulness meditation, you're equipping yourself with techniques to bring calm, clarity, and focus to your daily life. As you practice, you'll discover that the benefits extend far beyond the meditation cushion, helping you navigate the demands of work and life with greater ease.

Body Scan Meditation Technique

Body scans are a mindfulness practice that can significantly benefit busy professionals by enhancing their physical awareness and relaxation. In our fast-paced world, the connection between mind and body often gets lost in the chaos of daily responsibilities. By practising body scans, we can revive this vital connection, better understand our stress responses, and systematically relax different parts of our bodies.

Imagine your body as an intricate network of signals constantly communicating with you. Under stress, these signals may become muddled or go unnoticed altogether. Body scans help clear this communication pathway. By focusing on various body parts systematically, from head to toe or vice versa, one can identify tension, pain, or discomfort areas. This conscious attention promotes relaxation and helps in recognising how stress manifests physically. For example, professionals might find their shoulders habitually tense due to hours hunched over a computer. Acknowledging this allows them to address it through targeted relaxation techniques.

The beauty of body scan meditation lies in its simplicity and accessibility. It caters to all experience levels, making it an inclusive practice. Here's how you can get started:

1. Get Comfortable:

- Find a quiet, peaceful space where you won't be disturbed. Lying down is ideal, especially if you practice before sleep, as it allows for complete relaxation. If lying down isn't an option, sitting comfortably in a chair or on the floor also works well.
- Ensure your body is in a relaxed position, with your hands resting gently at your sides or on your lap.

2. Take Deep Breaths:

- Begin by slowing down your breathing. Inhale deeply from your abdomen rather than your chest and imagine filling your belly like a balloon with each breath.
- Focus on deep, slow breaths. These help calm your nervous system and bring your awareness fully to the present moment.

3. Bring Awareness to Your Feet:

- Start the body scan by directing your attention to your feet. Notice any sensations, such as warmth, coolness, or tension. Acknowledge them without judgment, whether they are strong or subtle.

- Take a few deep breaths and visualise the breath reaching down into your feet, helping you relax them more fully.

4. Scan Your Body:

- Gradually move your focus upwards, directing your attention to each area of the body. Start with your ankles, then your calves, knees, thighs, and so on, until you reach the top of your head.
- Spend time observing any sensations in each body part. If you encounter areas of tension, discomfort, or pain, focus your breath on those areas. As you breathe, imagine the tension dissipating with each exhale, creating a sense of release and relaxation.
- Continue this process slowly, ensuring you're fully present with each body part before moving on.

Benefits of Regular Practice:

- Reduces Stress and Anxiety: Body scan meditation helps activate the parasympathetic nervous system, promoting relaxation and reducing stress and anxiety. Focusing on bodily sensations also helps to bring your awareness away from worrying thoughts.
- Improves Body Awareness: Regular practice enhances your ability to tune into your body's sensations,

helping you become more aware of areas where you may be holding tension or stress. This awareness can lead to better physical and emotional well-being.

- Promotes Relaxation and Better Sleep: Practicing body scan meditation before sleep can help calm the mind and relax the body, improving sleep quality.
- Supports Emotional Regulation: By developing the ability to observe sensations without judgment, you cultivate emotional resilience, allowing you to respond to emotions with greater balance and control.

Research by Raypole concluded that this simple and accessible practice, suitable for all experience levels, helps you reconnect with your body, calm your mind, and foster greater mindfulness and relaxation through a clear, step-by-step approach that provides a structured method anyone can follow, regardless of their meditation experience.

Building Emotional Resilience with Body Scans

Regular body scan practice can be a powerful way to build resilience against high-stress situations, almost like strengthening emotional muscles. Think of body scans as your internal check-in, a way to detect and manage stress before it spirals out of control. By consistently tuning into your body, you heighten your self-awareness, creating an early warning system for emotional and physical tension. This increased awareness helps you recognise signs of stress, such as irritability or anxiety and allows you to take quick, restorative action.

Imagine you're in the middle of a marathon workday, racing between meetings, responding to emails, and suddenly feeling overwhelmed. Taking just five minutes for a body scan can be like hitting a reset button, clearing your mind and rejuvenating your energy. The same can be true when transitioning from work to personal life — a body scan can help you leave behind the day's stress, making it easier to be present and relaxed in your personal time.

But body scans offer more than immediate relief from stress; they promote long-term well-being. With consistent practice, you may experience benefits such as lower blood pressure, better sleep, and enhanced self-awareness. For example, many professionals struggle with insomnia due to racing thoughts at night. Research according to Scott shows that a body scan before bed can calm the mind and help you drift into restful sleep.

Another reason body scans are such an effective tool is their adaptability. They require no special equipment, can be done almost anywhere, and only take a few minutes — perfect for fitting into the busy lives of professionals. Whether at your desk, on a lunch break, or winding down at home, you can easily incorporate a quick scan to manage stress and maintain balance. Even a two-minute scan focusing on common stress hotspots like the neck, shoulders, and lower back can provide immediate relief.

Building a Consistent Meditation Habit

Creating and maintaining a regular meditation practice, especially for busy professionals, can initially feel challenging. However, with the right approach, it's entirely doable and can significantly support your emotional well-being. The key lies in finding a rhythm that fits your busy schedule, making meditation a sustainable part of your daily life.

Designate Specific Time Slots for Meditation

Just like you would with important meetings or project deadlines, scheduling dedicated time slots for meditation is essential. By structuring your practice this way, you ensure consistency, allowing meditation to become a natural part of your routine. Early mornings or late evenings are often ideal since these times offer quiet moments with fewer distractions. Set reminders on your phone or use calendar alerts to stay on track.

Start small. Five minutes a day is a good starting point. Over time, you can gradually increase the duration as you grow more comfortable with the practice. This incremental approach helps make meditation feel less overwhelming and helps build consistency, which is where the long-term benefits come from.

Acknowledge and Address Obstacles

The busyness of professional life is often the biggest challenge to maintaining a meditation routine. But instead of viewing it as a barrier, see it as an opportunity to integrate mindfulness into your day. Take mindful breaths while waiting for your computer to boot up or do a quick body scan during lunch. These micro-moments of mindfulness add up over time and can develop into a robust meditation practice.

Recognising the challenges a demanding work environment poses is the first step toward finding creative solutions. These mini-meditations are brief, but their cumulative impact can be significant.

Keep a Journal of Your Meditation Experience

Keeping a journal can help you deepen your mindfulness practice. Write down how you felt before, during, and after each meditation session. Track any distractions, emotional shifts, or mental clarity you noticed. By reflecting on these entries, you can see how your practice is evolving over time, even on days when it feels stagnant. It's like having a personal growth chart for your mind — seeing those small positive shifts written down can be incredibly motivating.

Engage Peers in Meditation

Meditating with others can foster a supportive environment, whether at work or in your personal life. Invite colleagues to join you for a few mindful minutes before a meeting or consider starting a workplace meditation group. These small initiatives promote well-being and can also improve team performance. Imagine starting a meeting with everyone feeling calm, centred, and focused. It would dramatically enhance both productivity and the quality of communication.

As managers and team leaders, encouraging these practices can create a culture of mindfulness, benefiting not just individuals but the organisation as a whole.

The Benefits of Regular Meditation

Extensive research supports the numerous benefits of meditation, both for mental and physical health. As an example, a study by Behan showed that mindfulness-based interventions like MBSR (Mindfulness-Based Stress Reduction) and MBCT (Mindfulness-Based Cognitive Therapy) significantly reduce anxiety, depression, and stress. For professionals in high-pressure environments, regular meditation leads to improved decision-making, better emotional regulation, and resilience under stress.

On a physiological level, meditation helps reduce cortisol, the body's primary stress hormone and lowers blood pressure. This improves your ability to manage stress and enhances your overall health and well-being. The cumulative effect of regular meditation means that with consistent practice, you're not just handling stress better — you're improving your long-term physical and mental health.

Additionally, chronically high levels of cortisol have been linked to accelerated aging due to factors like increased inflammation, oxidative stress, and damage to tissues, including the skin and brain. Over time, this can lead to conditions associated with aging, such as wrinkles, memory decline, and weakened immune function.

Incorporating Mindful Breaks into Daily Life

Mindful breaks — whether through brief body scans, breathing exercises, or focused meditation sessions — allow you to take control of your emotional state and manage stress proactively and healthily. These small, intentional pauses can make a world of difference in how you navigate high-pressure environments. With consistent practice, these tools help you approach challenges with greater clarity, ease, and resilience.

Practical Guidelines to Build Your Meditation Habit

To help you along your meditation journey, here are some guidelines:

- Designated Time Slots: Set aside specific times each day for meditation, just as you would for meetings. Begin with short sessions, such as five minutes, and gradually increase the duration as you become more comfortable.
- Use of Reminders: Leverage technology — smartphone alarms or app notifications can remind

you of your scheduled meditation times, keeping you accountable.

- Achievable Goals: Start with realistic objectives. Don't aim for an hour of meditation if you're just starting. Small, incremental progress is key to long-term success.
- Journal Keeping: Maintain a log of your meditation sessions. Note how you feel, what distractions arise, and any shifts in your mental state. Reflecting on these notes can help you track your progress and stay motivated.
- Peer Engagement: Engage colleagues or friends in your meditation journey. Meditate together or share experiences to build a support network. You could even start a meditation group at work for collective well-being.
- Micro-Moments: Incorporate brief moments of mindfulness into your day to day activities. Focus on your breath while commuting or do a quick body scan during work breaks.
- Utilise Apps: Guided meditation apps like Headspace, Calm, or Insight Timer offer structured sessions that fit perfectly into short breaks, helping you stay consistent and on track.

By integrating these practices into your daily routine, you'll discover that meditation isn't just another task to check off your to-do list. It's a tool to help you manage stress, boost your mental clarity, and enhance your overall well-being — one mindful breath at a time.

Key Takeaways

In this chapter, we've taken a closer look at various mindfulness meditation practices tailored for busy professionals. Let's recap the key insights:

- Understanding Mindfulness and Meditation:
    - Mindfulness is being present and aware in the moment
    - Meditation is a structured practice of training the mind
    - The two complement each other but are distinct practices
- Guided Meditations for Beginners:
    - Provide structure and ease the entry into mindfulness practice
    - Utilise apps and resources like Insight Timer, Headspace, or Calm
    - Set intentions to anchor your practice and give it purpose
    - Short, frequent sessions are often more effective than longer, intermittent ones
- Silent Meditation Practices:

- o Foster deeper self-reliance and personal exploration
- o Create a clutter-free, peaceful environment for practice
- o Start with brief periods and gradually increase the duration
- o Practice observing thoughts without engaging with them
- Body Scan Meditation Technique:
  - o Enhances physical awareness and relaxation
  - o Helps identify areas of tension and stress in the body
  - o Can be practiced in various settings and durations
  - o Promotes overall well-being and stress reduction
- Building a Consistent Meditation Habit:
  - o Designate specific time slots for meditation
  - o Set achievable goals and use reminders
  - o Keep a journal to track progress and insights
  - o Engage peers and create a supportive environment
  - o Incorporate micro-moments of mindfulness throughout the day

Remember, meditation is not about mastery but about being present and cultivating awareness. As you integrate these practices into your professional life, be patient with yourself and approach it with curiosity rather than judgment. The benefits of regular mindfulness meditation, including reduced stress, improved focus, and enhanced emotional regulation, can significantly improve your professional performance and personal well-being.

By making mindfulness a part of your daily routine, you're investing in a powerful tool to help you navigate the challenges of a high-pressure career with greater ease and clarity. Whether through guided sessions, silent meditation, body scans, or brief moments of mindfulness throughout your day, each practice contributes to building a more resilient, focused, and balanced professional self.

Chapter 7: Building Emotional Resilience

> *Between stimulus and response, there is a space. In that space is our power to choose our response. In our response lies our growth and our freedom.*
>
> — *Viktor E. Frankl*

Let's dive into understanding emotional triggers — those moments that turn you from calm and collected into an emotional volcano on the verge of eruption. We're not just identifying the issues; we're equipping you with tools to recognise and manage these triggers before they blow. You'll learn to spot the patterns, reflect on your responses, and keep an emotional inventory that will serve as a map to guide you through turbulent times. These tools are more than just tips; they are the ingredients for transforming stress into manageable, bite-sized pieces.

Understanding Emotional Triggers

In high-pressure careers, professionals are often exposed to situations that trigger intense emotions, making it crucial to identify and understand these emotional triggers. Recognising what provokes a strong emotional response is the first step toward managing reactions and maintaining composure under stress. By gaining this self-awareness, you can better control your emotions, enhancing your resilience and overall effectiveness.

Proactively managing emotional triggers equips you with the tools to navigate your career's complexities more efficiently, allowing you to approach challenges with greater focus and energy. Emotional resilience is not about eliminating stress but learning to handle it more effectively. By developing awareness, reflecting on experiences, and mapping your emotional landscape, you'll be well-prepared to face difficult situations, whether a tight deadline or a tense conversation with a colleague.

Our emotional wellness toolkit comprises 4 components: awareness, reflection, mapping, and inventory.

Identifying Common Triggers

Let's start with the basics: what exactly are emotional triggers? Triggers are specific situations, interactions, or people that provoke an intense emotional response. For many professionals, these might include high-stakes meetings, critical feedback, tight deadlines, or interpersonal conflicts. By identifying these situations, you gain awareness of when you're most likely to experience heightened emotions.

For instance, let's say you notice you always feel anxious when receiving critical feedback. This awareness allows you to mentally prepare for such situations, knowing that feedback triggers your anxiety. Next time a performance review approaches, you might tell yourself, "I tend to get anxious during these reviews. Now that I'm aware of this, I can take a deep breath and focus on listening constructively."

Here are some practical steps to help guide you through the process:

1. Self-Monitoring: Pay Attention to Your Reactions

- Objective: Become more aware of how your body and emotions react to different situations.
- Steps:
  - Physical Reactions: Notice physical signs of emotional distress or discomfort, such as a racing heart, clenched fists, or shallow breathing. These can be cues that your emotions are being triggered.
  - Emotional Reactions: Pay close attention to your feelings during various situations — anger, frustration, sadness, anxiety, or excitement. Try to label each emotion as it arises to better understand what you're experiencing (not in a judgemental way).
  - Mindfulness: Practice staying present and mindful throughout the day. Regularly check in with yourself during moments of stress or conflict to monitor how your emotions shift.

- Journaling: Keep a journal or use a note-taking app to jot down moments of emotional discomfort or overreaction. Note what happened, how you felt, and what you think triggered that response. Over time, this record will help you identify patterns.

2. Note Patterns: Track Emotional Triggers

- Objective: Identify specific situations or recurring themes that lead to emotional responses.
- Steps:
    - Situational Triggers: Look for common situations that spark strong emotional responses. These may include deadlines, personal criticism, conflict, or particular environments.
    - People Triggers: Reflect on whether specific people or types of interactions consistently evoke emotional reactions. For instance, do you often feel anxious or defensive around authority figures or in social situations?
    - Themes: As you track your emotional responses, certain themes may emerge, such as feelings of inadequacy or rejection. Identifying these can help you recognise underlying issues that need attention.

- Long-term Patterns: Over time, patterns of triggers can provide insight into unresolved emotional issues, such as insecurity or past trauma, that continue to influence your reactions.

3. Ask for Feedback: Gain Perspective from Others

- Objective: Get an outside perspective on your emotional triggers, especially ones you may not recognise.
- Steps:
    - Trusted Individuals: Ask close friends, family members, or colleagues for feedback on how you react in certain situations. Sometimes, others can spot emotional triggers you may not be fully aware of, such as becoming defensive or shutting down during certain conversations.
    - Specific Examples: When asking for feedback, provide specific instances where you felt emotionally triggered, and ask for their observations. Did they notice a particular shift in your behaviour, tone, or body language?
    - Therapist or Counsellor: A trained therapist can be particularly helpful in identifying emotional triggers and understanding how past experiences influence current reactions. They

can provide structured techniques for managing triggers more effectively.
- o Reflecting on Feedback: When you receive feedback, reflect on it with an open mind. Even if it feels uncomfortable, recognising blind spots is a key step in building emotional resilience.

Benefits of Regular Practice:

- Improved Emotional Awareness: By monitoring your physical and emotional responses, you'll become more aware of your triggers, which allows you to manage them more effectively.
- Greater Emotional Control: Identifying patterns helps you anticipate and prepare for situations that could trigger strong emotions, giving you more control over your reactions.
- Strengthened Relationships: Asking for feedback and being open to others' perspectives can improve communication and strengthen relationships as you become more attuned to how your emotions affect others.
- Enhanced Problem-Solving: Understanding emotional triggers allows you to address the root causes of distress, helping you develop coping strategies that increase resilience in challenging situations.

Building emotional resilience through self-monitoring, pattern recognition, and feedback is a gradual process that empowers you to better manage emotions and maintain mental well-being during stressful situations.

Reflecting on Responses

Once you've identified your triggers, the next step is to reflect on how they affect your responses. This is where introspection comes into play. After a triggering event, take a moment to analyse your reaction. Did you become defensive? Angry? Overwhelmed? Reflect on how these emotions influenced your behaviour and decision-making.

Self-reflection is like holding a mini-therapy session with yourself. For example, if you realise you often snap at colleagues when stressed, ask yourself why. Perhaps you're feeling unsupported or overwhelmed. Acknowledging this can help you develop healthier coping methods, like delegating tasks or asking for assistance.

Here are some practical steps to help guide you through the process:

1. Pause and Reflect:

- Objective: Clarify your emotional reactions by assessing what triggered them and how you reacted.
- Steps:
    - Create Space: After experiencing an emotional reaction — whether it's frustration, sadness, or

anger — pause and give yourself a moment to breathe. This brief moment of detachment helps you break the automatic, habitual reaction cycle.
- Reflect on the Situation: Ask yourself questions like, "What just happened?" and "Why did I respond this way?" Focus on understanding what external event or internal thought triggered your emotional response.
- Assess Your Reaction: Consider whether your response matched the situation. Did you overreact, underreact, or respond appropriately? This helps you understand whether your reaction was driven more by the trigger or underlying emotional patterns.

2. Journal It:

- Objective: Use journaling as a tool to explore your emotions and reactions in more depth and help uncover patterns and root causes.
- Steps:
  - Daily Journaling: Dedicate a few minutes each day or after significant emotional events to jot down your thoughts. Include details about what happened, how you felt, and what you think triggered your response.

- Structure Your Thoughts: Use prompts like "What triggered this emotion?", "What was my immediate reaction?" and "How did my body feel?" to guide your journaling. This makes the process more focused and helps uncover specific patterns or triggers.
- Track Emotional Patterns: Over time, review your entries to identify recurring emotional triggers or situations where you tend to react similarly. This insight can help you anticipate triggers and respond differently in the future.

3. Seek Insights:

- Objective: Discuss your emotional responses with a trusted friend, mentor, or therapist to gain additional perspectives.
- Steps:
  - Choose a Trusted Person: Select someone you trust who can offer objective insights. This could be a close friend, family member, or mentor who knows you well or a professional like a therapist or counsellor.
  - Share Your Reflections: When discussing your reflections, be open about the emotional reactions you've experienced and the triggers you've identified. Sharing your experiences

often helps you gain clarity and recognise blind spots you might have missed.
- Ask for Feedback: Request feedback on how they perceive your emotional responses. They may notice patterns in your behaviour that you hadn't identified yourself. Ask them if they've observed how you handle stress, anger, or sadness and whether your reactions seem proportional to the situation.
- Apply New Insights: Use this feedback to refine your self-awareness. Insights from others can help you develop more balanced reactions and make you more mindful of how your emotions impact your actions.

Benefits of Regular Practice:

- Improved Self-Awareness: Reflecting on emotional responses helps you understand your triggers and reactions, increasing your emotional intelligence and resilience.
- Emotional Balance: Recognising your patterns can equip you to manage emotions better, reducing the likelihood of overreacting in stressful situations.
- Enhanced Communication: Discussing your reflections with others promotes open communication and fosters a supportive environment, encouraging healthier emotional interactions.

- Better Decision-Making: Pausing and reflecting before reacting allows for more thoughtful responses, reducing impulsive emotional decisions that could harm relationships or create unnecessary stress.

Regularly practising these steps — pausing to reflect, journaling your thoughts, and seeking insights — will gradually build emotional resilience, empowering you to better understand and manage your emotional triggers.

Mapping Emotional Currents

No self-respecting management consultant would do an analysis without creating some charts.

Charting your emotions is a visual exercise that helps you track your emotional responses over time. Imagine plotting your emotions on a chart where the x-axis represents time and the y-axis represents the intensity of your emotions. By mapping out your emotional highs and lows in response to different situations, you can identify patterns.

For example, if you notice that Monday mornings are consistently tough because of weekend work dread, visualise that spike in anxiety on your chart. Once you recognise the pattern, you can take proactive steps, like scheduling a relaxing activity on Sunday night or starting Monday with lighter tasks.

1. Chart Your Emotions: Use a Visual Tool

- Objective: Create a visual representation of your emotional experiences over a period of time to better understand the flow of your emotions.
- Steps:
    - Choose a Tracking Method: Use a journal, a graph, or an app designed for emotional tracking. A simple approach is to create a daily chart with emotional "intensity" on one axis and time on the other. You can rate your emotional states from 1 (very low) to 10 (very high) for each day.
    - Log Your Emotions: Record how you feel regularly throughout the day (e.g., morning, midday, evening). Write down or input your emotions, focusing on both positive and negative feelings. You can use emotion categories like happiness, frustration, stress, calm, or anxiety to help with tracking.
    - Look for Triggers: Alongside your emotional rating, note any events, situations, or interactions that you believe contributed to each emotional state. This helps link emotions to external or internal triggers.

2. Identify Peaks and Valleys: Look for Patterns

- Objective: Analyse your emotional chart to identify patterns, such as high and low points in your emotional responses.
- Steps:
    - Review Weekly Trends: At the end of each week, review your chart and look for emotional "peaks" (periods of intense emotions) and "valleys" (times when emotions were low or neutral). Are there any patterns that consistently affect your emotional state, such as a particular time of day or specific situations?
    - Link to Triggers: Identify the common triggers for each peak or valley that led to those emotions. For example, do you experience high levels of stress on Mondays because of work meetings, or do you feel calm during your evening walks? Recognising these triggers helps you understand how certain events or habits influence your emotional well-being.
    - Analyse Emotional Stability: Pay attention to whether your emotional reactions are balanced or if you frequently experience extreme highs or lows. This information can help you identify areas where emotional regulation may need attention.

3. Adjust Accordingly: Modify Your Routine

- Objective: Use the insights from your emotional map to make practical changes to your routine and reduce emotional stress during high-intensity periods.
- Steps:
  - Plan Around Peaks: If you identify specific times when your emotions spike (e.g., during work deadlines or stressful meetings), adjust your schedule to manage or minimise stress during those periods. For instance, you might incorporate calming activities like deep breathing or meditation before known stressors.
  - Introduce Positive Habits: If you notice that certain activities or habits improve your emotional state (e.g., exercise, mindfulness practices, or time with friends), incorporate more of these into your daily routine to maintain emotional balance.
  - Avoid Emotional Triggers: If possible, limit exposure to recurring triggers that lead to negative emotions. If you can't avoid them, prepare in advance by practising emotional regulation techniques like mindful breathing or taking breaks during high-stress periods.

- Set Goals for Emotional Health: Use your emotional map as a guide to set goals for improving emotional resilience. For example, if your chart reveals consistent anxiety in the mornings, make it a goal to implement a calming morning routine, such as journaling or mindful breathing.

Benefits of Regular Practice:

- Improved Emotional Awareness: Mapping your emotions helps you visualise and better understand the ebb and flow of your feelings, making it easier to recognise patterns and triggers.
- Enhanced Emotional Control: By identifying emotional peaks and valleys, you can anticipate potential emotional challenges and prepare to manage them effectively.
- Personalised Stress Management: Adjusting your routine based on your emotional map allows for a more personalised approach to managing stress and maintaining emotional balance.
- Long-term Emotional Growth. Over time, regular mapping can help you develop deeper emotional resilience as you gain a clearer understanding of how to navigate emotional highs and lows.

You will gain valuable insights into your emotional landscape by consistently practising these steps. This will allow you to modify your habits and better manage your emotions over time.

Creating an Emotional Inventory

Another helpful strategy is keeping an emotional inventory. This involves regularly recording your emotional experiences, noting what triggered them and how you responded. Over time, your emotional inventory becomes a valuable tool for identifying recurring patterns and gaining a deeper understanding of your emotional landscape.

Consider keeping a journal where you jot down daily emotional highs and lows. Reflect on what triggered the emotions and how you handled them. After a few weeks, you might notice specific people or tasks that consistently trigger negative feelings. You can develop strategies to navigate these situations more effectively with this insight.

By following these guidelines, you'll be well on your way to better understanding your emotional triggers and building emotional resilience. This proactive approach will help you navigate stressful situations with greater composure and focus, giving you more energy to tackle challenges head-on.

1. Daily Entries: Make It a Habit to Document Your Emotional Experiences

- Objective: Track your emotions regularly to increase awareness of your emotional patterns and triggers.
- Steps:

- Set a Routine: Choose a specific time to write down your emotional experiences each day. This could be in the morning to reflect on the previous day or in the evening to capture how you felt throughout the day. Keeping a consistent routine helps you stay engaged with the practice.
   - Use a Simple Format: Your entries don't need to be lengthy. A few sentences summarising how you felt and what happened is enough. For example, "I felt anxious during my meeting this afternoon," or "I was happy and relaxed after my evening walk."
   - Record Emotional Intensity: In addition to describing your emotions, you can assign an intensity score on a scale of 1-10 to help you track how strongly you felt these emotions.
   - Track Physical Reactions: Include any physical responses to emotions (e.g., tense shoulders, racing heart), as they are important clues to how emotions manifest in your body.

2. Detail Specifics: Include What Triggered the Emotion and How You Responded

- Objective: Identify emotional triggers and your automatic responses to better understand your emotional habits.

- Steps:
    - Identify Triggers: When documenting your emotions, always specify what event or thought triggered that emotion. Triggers could be external (e.g., a stressful work meeting) or internal (e.g., an anxious thought or memory).
    - Describe Your Response: Reflect on how you reacted emotionally, mentally, and physically. Did you withdraw, become irritable, or take deep breaths to calm down? Understanding your reactions helps you see where your emotional regulation is effective and where it might need improvement.
    - Note Coping Mechanisms: Record any strategies you used to manage your emotions, such as mindfulness exercises, taking a walk, or talking to someone about how you felt. This helps you see what works best in handling emotional triggers.

3. Review Regularly: Periodically Review Your Entries to Identify Recurring Themes or Triggers

- Objective: Analyse your emotional inventory to spot patterns, emotional triggers, and areas for improvement.
- Steps:

- Weekly or Monthly Review: Set aside time to review your entries regularly. Look back at the week or month and reflect on recurring emotions, common triggers, or patterns of reaction. For instance, you may notice that stress at work triggers anxiety on Mondays or that social events make you feel energised or overwhelmed.
- Spot Emotional Trends: Pay attention to patterns of emotional highs and lows. For example, are there specific days of the week, types of interactions, or activities that consistently evoke certain emotions? Identifying these trends will help you anticipate emotional reactions and adjust accordingly.
- Assess Progress: During your review, assess whether you've improved at managing certain emotional triggers or if some areas still need work. Reflect on whether your coping strategies have improved and which ones are most effective.
- Adjust Your Approach: Based on your observations, adjust your coping mechanisms or try new strategies to manage your emotional responses. For example, if you notice you often feel irritable in the afternoon, you might

incorporate a short break or mindfulness exercise to help manage that emotion before it escalates.

Benefits of Regular Practice:

- Increased Emotional Awareness: Keeping a daily emotional inventory helps you stay more attuned to your emotions and what triggers them, allowing you to address emotional challenges with greater insight.
- Better Emotional Management: By regularly reviewing your entries, you develop the ability to anticipate and prepare for triggers, reducing the likelihood of being caught off guard by emotional responses.
- Improved Coping Strategies: Tracking your responses and reviewing what works allows you to refine your coping mechanisms over time, leading to healthier emotional regulation.
- Long-Term Emotional Resilience: Consistently documenting and reflecting on your emotions promotes emotional resilience by helping you better understand and manage your emotional landscape.

By making daily entries, detailing emotional triggers and responses, and regularly reviewing your emotional inventory, you will gradually build emotional resilience and become better equipped to manage your emotional well-being.

A brief note on journalling

I appreciate that mindful journaling may feel cabbalistic to many and, therefore, underutilised or ignored, but substantial empirical evidence supports its emotional wellness benefits.

Research has shown that journaling, particularly when combined with mindfulness practices, can help reduce symptoms of anxiety, stress, and depression. It enables individuals to process emotions, prioritise concerns, and gain clarity, ultimately improving emotional regulation and self-awareness.

For instance, studies indicate that regular journaling can lead to a reduction in depressive thoughts and an improvement in mood, similar to the effects of cognitive-behavioural therapy in certain cases. Another review of research found that journaling about emotions or personal experiences has been effective in helping individuals manage mental health conditions such as PTSD, anxiety, and depression.

Additionally, journaling can enhance self-reflection and foster gratitude, both of which are linked to greater emotional well-being.

If you are interested in finding out more, I have provided some of the research in the reference section at the back of this book. Look for 1) Baikie and Wilhelm, 2) Hasanzadeh, Khoshknab, and Norozi, 3) Sohal, Kim-Godwin and Gazadinda, and 4) Stice, Burton, Bearman, and Rohde.

Practices for Emotional Self-Regulation

Effectively managing emotional triggers requires more than just awareness; it calls for practical tools to regulate emotional responses. Here are some key practices for building emotional resilience.

Mindful Breathing Techniques

Mindful breathing is a deceptively simple but powerful tool for managing emotional states. Our thoughts can scatter in high-pressure situations, leading to stress and diminished performance. A helpful practice is breath counting: sit calmly, close your eyes, and focus on counting your breaths — inhaling for five counts, exhaling for seven. This simple exercise shifts your attention from stressors to the steady rhythm of your breath, helping to ground you.

Physical cues can also help you ground yourself. Try placing one hand on your chest and the other on your abdomen, feeling the rise and fall of your breath. Chowdhury discusses how this tactile feedback helps anchor you physically and mentally, keeping you focused on the present.

Cognitive Reappraisal

Negative experiences are inevitable in high-stress careers, but how you interpret them can significantly influence your emotional resilience. Cognitive reappraisal is the practice of reframing negative situations to alter their emotional impact. Instead of viewing critical feedback as a personal failure, consider it an opportunity for growth. Research shows that this technique reduces the intensity of negative emotions and improves emotional responses over time.

Physical Movement

Stress can often manifest as tension in the body, so physical movement is another effective strategy for emotional regulation. Activities like jogging, yoga, or even a brisk walk can release endorphins, boost mood, and provide mental clarity. Physical exercise also serves as an emotional catharsis, allowing you to vent built-up energy and stress. When you're having a particularly rough day, consider taking a break for some light stretching or a walk to refresh both body and mind.

Scheduled Reflection Time

In the whirlwind of daily responsibilities, it's easy to let emotions go unexamined. Setting aside specific times for reflection can help you process your emotions more effectively. Even ten minutes at the end of the day to journal about your feelings can reveal patterns in your emotional responses. This regular reflection makes it easier to anticipate and manage triggers in the future.

Blending These Strategies for Greater Emotional Resilience

Building emotional resilience is about combining multiple strategies to create a balanced framework for managing stress. Start small — maybe with mindful breathing every morning or cognitive reappraisal during tough feedback sessions. As you become more comfortable, you can gradually incorporate physical activity and scheduled reflection times.

The goal is to develop a system that works for you. By blending these techniques, you'll build a robust emotional toolkit that allows you to navigate even the toughest days with composure and clarity. These practices aren't about avoiding stress altogether — they're about learning to handle stress more effectively and, ultimately, fostering long-term emotional resilience.

The Role of Compassion in Resilience

Nurturing compassion — for yourself and others — is a powerful tool for building emotional resilience, especially in high-stress professional environments. With the pressures of tight deadlines, demanding clients, and constant challenges, compassion can act as a buffer, helping you maintain mental well-being and manage stress more effectively. These practices aren't just feel-good extras; they're game changers.

Self-Compassion Practices

One of the most crucial components of emotional resilience is self-compassion. Mistakes in fast-paced, high-stakes careers are inevitable, but how you respond to them can fuel or diminish your resilience. Too often, professionals meet their errors with harsh self-criticism, leading to increased stress and lower performance. Practising self-compassion means treating yourself with the same kindness and understanding you would offer a friend.

Research by Garcia et al. links self-compassion with higher levels of well-being and improved professional quality of life. To cultivate this, professionals can engage in mindful self-care routines. Mindfulness helps recognise internal needs and respond to them with deliberate care. For instance, instead of dwelling on a mistake, you might pause, acknowledge the discomfort, and choose a self-care activity that promotes relaxation and clarity, such as deep breathing or taking a short walk. By incorporating these moments of self-kindness into your daily routine, you build resilience and bounce back more quickly after setbacks.

- Steps:
    - Acknowledge Mistakes Without Judgment: Recognise errors without harsh self-criticism. Treat yourself with the same kindness you'd offer a friend.
    - Engage in Mindful Activities: Practice mindfulness, such as meditation or journaling, to help ground yourself and centre your thoughts.
    - Prioritise Self-Care Routines: Schedule regular self-care activities — such as exercise, hobbies,

or relaxation techniques — to maintain physical and mental well-being.

Compassionate Listening

In professional settings, giving your full attention to others' emotions is a critical skill that fosters a supportive work environment. Compassionate listening goes beyond merely hearing words — it's about deeply understanding the speaker's emotional state and offering empathy. This skill is vital for creating safe spaces where colleagues feel heard and valued, which can enhance teamwork and resilience.

Compassionate listening requires setting aside distractions, being fully present in conversations, and validating the speaker's emotions. By practising this skill, you can strengthen connections and foster a more collaborative, emotionally resilient work environment.

- Steps:
    - Be Present in Conversations: Remove distractions and give your full attention to the speaker. Show empathy through body language and active listening.
    - Validate Emotions: Acknowledge the speaker's feelings without jumping to solutions or dismissals.
    - Foster Open Communication: Create a culture that encourages sharing emotions and

concerns, making it safe for people to express themselves.

Creating Compassionate Workspaces

Building a compassionate workspace can significantly reduce stress and boost resilience across teams. Compassionate work environments are characterised by mutual respect, open communication, and support among team members. When employees feel that their emotional well-being is valued, they are better equipped to handle professional pressures and challenges.

Leaders play a pivotal role in creating these environments. First, they can encourage open communication by promoting regular check-ins and feedback sessions where team members can share their experiences without fear of judgment. Second, implementing policies that prioritise employee well-being — such as flexible work arrangements and access to mental health resources — demonstrates a commitment to compassion.

A great example is introducing initiatives like "Wellness Wednesdays," where employees participate in stress-relief activities such as meditation or group exercises. These practices provide immediate stress relief and signal to employees that their emotional health matters, leading to increased resilience and higher employee satisfaction. This culture of support also helps attract and retain top talent, creating a more engaged and loyal workforce.

- Steps:
    - Promote Open Dialogue: Implement regular check-ins and feedback sessions to encourage open, transparent communication.
    - Introduce Well-Being Policies: Offer flexible work options and provide access to mental health resources.
    - Organise Team-Building Activities: Host group exercises, social events, or wellness programs that promote collaboration and mutual support.

Practicing Gratitude

Incorporating gratitude into daily life is another powerful way to boost emotional resilience. Gratitude shifts your focus from stress and what's lacking to what's positive and fulfilling in your life. This simple shift in perspective can counterbalance the negative effects of high-pressure environments and improve your overall well-being.

One effective way to practice gratitude is by keeping a gratitude journal. Spend a few minutes each day writing down things you're grateful for, such as supportive colleagues, recent successes, or personal milestones. Even small things, like a pleasant conversation or a good cup of coffee, can shift your mindset. Additionally, expressing gratitude to others — whether through a thank you note or verbal appreciation —

can strengthen relationships and create a positive ripple effect throughout the workplace.

- Steps:
    - Keep a Gratitude Journal: Write down three things you're thankful for each day to cultivate a more positive mindset.
    - Express Gratitude to Others: Regularly thank colleagues for their contributions and support, either verbally or through notes.
    - Incorporate Collective Gratitude: Start meetings or team activities with expressions of gratitude to build a positive and appreciative work culture.

A brief note on practicing gratitude

Much like journalling, the concept of practicing gratitude and keeping a gratitude journal may seem like skirting the fringes of voodoo, so I want to provide some scientific evidence to backup the value of this practice.

Practicing gratitude and keeping a gratitude journal have been subjects of numerous scientific studies, which have demonstrated several benefits for mental health and well-being. Research has consistently shown that cultivating gratitude can lead to increased happiness, improved relationships, and better overall life satisfaction.

Some key benefits that have been scientifically proven include reduced depression and anxiety symptoms, improved sleep quality, and enhanced resilience to stress. A study by Emmons and McCullough found that participants who kept gratitude journals reported feeling more optimistic and better about their lives compared to those who didn't. Additionally, research by Wood et al. indicated that gratitude is associated with lower levels of stress and depression.

Practicing gratitude can be particularly beneficial for individuals in high-pressure jobs like management consulting. The fast-paced, demanding nature of consulting work often leads to stress, burnout, and decreased job satisfaction. Incorporating gratitude practices can help consultants maintain a positive perspective and improve their resilience in the face of challenging projects and long hours.

A study by Cheng et al. found that gratitude was positively associated with job satisfaction and negatively associated with job stress among healthcare professionals, a finding that may extend to other high-stress professions like consulting. For management consultants specifically, cultivating gratitude could help in maintaining client relationships, fostering team cohesion, and enhancing problem-solving skills by promoting a more positive and open mindset. Regular gratitude practice may also aid in work-life balance by encouraging consultants to appreciate aspects of their personal lives, potentially reducing the risk of work-related burnout.

Creating a Supportive Environment

In today's fast-paced professional world, high-performing individuals often face immense pressure. A supportive work environment is crucial for helping them maintain resilience and performance. By fostering compassion and trust among colleagues, creating spaces for open dialogue, and encouraging authenticity, organisations can provide the psychological safety professionals need to thrive.

Cultivating Trust Among Peers

Trust is a cornerstone of a compassionate workplace. When team members trust each other, they feel safe enough to express emotions and concerns without fear of judgment. This open expression allows potential problems to be addressed early, preventing them from escalating. Transparency and open communication help build this trust, as does celebrating small wins and acknowledging each team member's contributions.

Encouraging Authenticity

Authenticity means creating an environment where people feel free to be themselves without fear of negative consequences. When individuals can be authentic, they reduce the cognitive load of maintaining a façade, which helps reduce stress and improve emotional resilience. Leaders can model this by sharing their own vulnerabilities, encouraging others to do the same, and embracing diversity in perspectives and backgrounds.

Implementing Regular Check-Ins

Regular emotional wellness check-ins can be a proactive way to maintain support among team members. These can take the form of one-on-one meetings, or group discussions focused on emotional well-being. By providing a dedicated space for employees to express concerns, share their emotional experiences, and receive support, regular check-ins help identify and address issues before they become more significant problems.

By integrating compassion into both individual practices and workplace culture, professionals can build emotional resilience and create environments where everyone feels supported, valued, and equipped to handle stress. Compassion isn't just a soft skill — it's a critical factor in thriving amidst professional challenges.

Key Takeaways

As we've discussed throughout this chapter there are various strategies for building emotional resilience in high-pressure professional environments. Let's recap the key insights:

- Understanding Emotional Triggers:
    - Identify common triggers in your work environment

- Reflect on your responses to these triggers
- Map emotional currents to visualise patterns over time
- Create an emotional inventory to track and understand your emotional landscape

• Practices for Emotional Self-Regulation:
- Utilise mindful breathing techniques to recentre and regain focus
- Apply cognitive reappraisal to reframe negative situations
- Incorporate physical movement into your routine for stress relief
- Schedule regular reflection time to process emotions

• The Role of Compassion in Resilience:
- Cultivate self-compassion through mindful self-care routines
- Practice compassionate listening to foster supportive exchanges
- Create compassionate workspaces that prioritise employee well-being
- Incorporate gratitude practices into daily reflections

• Creating a Supportive Environment:
- Cultivate trust among peers through transparency and celebration of achievements

- Encourage authenticity by allowing individuals to express their true selves
- Implement regular emotional wellness check-ins

By integrating these practices into your professional life, you can develop a robust emotional resilience that will serve you well in navigating the challenges of high-pressure careers. Remember, building resilience is an ongoing process that requires consistent effort and self-awareness.

Key takeaways:

- Emotional resilience is crucial for maintaining performance and well-being in demanding professions
- Understanding your emotional triggers is the first step towards better emotional management
- Self-regulation techniques, compassion practices, and a supportive environment all contribute to building resilience
- Regular practice and integration of these strategies into daily routines is essential for long-term benefits

As you move forward, consider which of these strategies resonate most with you and start incorporating them into your professional life. With time and practice, you'll find yourself better equipped to handle stress, maintain focus, and thrive in your high-performance career while safeguarding your emotional well-being.

Chapter 8: Mindfulness in Communication

> *Listening is an art that requires attention over talent, spirit over ego, others over self.*
>
> — *Dale Carnegie*

Mindfulness in communication may sound like a Zen master's guide to navigating professional emails, but it's much more than that — it's about making your workplace interactions more meaningful and less stressful. Imagine a world where every conversation felt productive, unlike a high-stakes negotiation or a game of corporate charades. That's the power of mindful communication.

This chapter dives into the art of active listening, helping you stay present and engaged rather than mentally ticking off your to do list while nodding politely. We'll explore how to spot non-verbal cues that communicate more than words alone, like when someone says they're "fine," but their body language says, "Help me!" You'll also learn reflective listening techniques, where simply paraphrasing someone's words can make you seem wise beyond your years. And finally, we'll talk about asking open-ended questions that can turn a dull meeting into a lively discussion.

Active Listening Skills

Active listening is the cornerstone of mindful communication. It's about fully engaging with the speaker, not just hearing their words but understanding their message and emotional state. Mastering this skill in the consulting world and in many other environments can greatly enhance workplace interactions.

The Art of Presence in Active Listening

The first step to active listening is being fully present. This means setting aside distractions — no checking emails or glancing at your phone — so you can give the speaker your undivided attention. In a fast-paced world where multitasking is often praised, being present can feel like a rare and valuable gift to the person speaking.

To practice being fully present, try setting specific times for uninterrupted meetings or conversations. For example, during team meetings, turn off notifications and focus entirely on what's being said. Making eye contact and nodding shows that you're genuinely engaged. This simple act of being present demonstrates respect and fosters a culture of mindfulness within your team.

Recognizing Verbal and Non-Verbal Cues

Communication isn't just about the words we use; it's also about how we say them. Recognising both verbal and non-verbal cues is essential for understanding the full message. For example, a colleague might say they're fine, but if their arms are crossed and their eyes are downcast, more may be going on.

Practice observing body language during conversations. Are they fidgeting? Do they lean in or away when speaking? Do their facial expressions match their words? Similarly, pay attention to tone of voice — a sudden change in pitch or speed can indicate excitement, anxiety, or frustration. Tuning into these signals allows you to respond with empathy and understanding, even when words aren't fully expressing the person's true feelings.

Reflective Listening for Validation

Reflective listening takes active listening to the next level. It involves paraphrasing or summarizing the speaker's words to show that you understand their point of view. Reflective listening validates the speaker's message, which can be especially helpful in resolving conflicts or clarifying complex issues.

For example, if a team member shares a concern about a tight deadline, you might respond with, "It sounds like the project timeline is stressing you out. Did I get that right?" This confirms your understanding and invites the speaker to clarify or expand on their thoughts. Reflective listening builds trust, ensuring that everyone feels heard and understood.

Asking Open-Ended Questions to Encourage Dialogue

Open-ended questions are an excellent way to foster deeper conversations. Instead of asking yes/no questions like, "Did you finish the report?" try something more engaging like, "What challenges did you face while working on the report?" This invites the speaker to share more information and helps uncover insights that may not have come up otherwise.

For example, in a performance review, you could ask, "What achievements are you most proud of this year, and where do you see room for improvement?" This encourages a more meaningful discussion and allows the employee to reflect on their growth. Asking open-ended questions deepens the conversation and fosters an environment of collaboration and continuous improvement.

Mindful Speech Practices

Mindful communication isn't just about listening; it's also about speaking with intention and clarity. How you communicate in high-pressure environments can foster collaboration or create tension. By practising mindful speech, you can enhance both clarity and connection in your workplace interactions.

Choosing Words Wisely

The words you choose significantly impact how your message is received. Thoughtful word selection can inspire action, motivate your team, or diffuse tension in stressful situations.

For instance, framing a project as "challenging" instead of "difficult" can shift the conversation from dread to excitement and possibility.

Using simple, direct language ensures that everyone understands your message clearly. Avoid jargon and complex phrases when simpler alternatives will do. The goal is to communicate your ideas in a way that resonates with your audience and motivates them to take action.

As management consultants, we are no strangers to bullshit bingo. For those of you who don't know what this is, it's the practice of spotting and calling out overused buzzwords and jargon that frequently pop up in corporate meetings and presentations. Words like "synergy," "paradigm shift," and "value-added" are often thrown around without much substance, masking real issues and hindering effective communication.

For example: "As we move forward with the synergistic integration of cross-functional capabilities, we need to leverage core competencies to optimise our value proposition, ensuring a paradigm shift that drives scalable, sustainable growth in a dynamic marketplace."

Or said another way, "We need to work together, using our strengths, to improve what we offer and grow steadily in a changing market."

Mindful communication, by cutting out jargon and buzzwords, helps foster clearer conversations and builds stronger relationships because people can focus on what's actually being said, making it easier to connect and understand each other.

Pacing and Tone of Voice

How you say something can be just as important as what you say. Speaking too quickly can overwhelm your audience, while speaking too slowly might cause them to lose interest. A balanced pace helps ensure your message is absorbed effectively. Additionally, your tone of voice is important in how your message is received. A warm, friendly tone can make difficult feedback feel supportive, while a harsh tone can lead to defensiveness.

Being mindful of your pacing and tone allows you to deliver your message with greater impact, fostering better understanding and collaboration.

Avoiding Assumptions

One of the biggest pitfalls in communication is making assumptions about what others know or think. Assumptions can lead to misunderstandings and gaps in communication. Instead, approach conversations with curiosity, seeking to fully understand the other person's perspective.

For example, when discussing a project's progress, don't assume that everyone is aware of the challenges that have arisen. Instead, say, "Let's review the challenges we've faced this week." This ensures that everyone is on the same page and opens up the conversation for meaningful dialogue.

Practicing Transparency

Honesty and transparency are key to building trust in the workplace. When you're clear and upfront, especially about difficult issues, you prevent misunderstandings and build a culture of openness. For instance, if a project deadline can't be met, acknowledging it early and explaining why fosters an environment of trust.

As a leader, being transparent helps set expectations and creates a supportive work environment. By saying, "We're behind schedule due to some unforeseen challenges, but we're working on solutions," you inform your team and demonstrate that challenges can be addressed together.

Approach difficult conversations with an open mind

When we go into conversations — especially difficult ones — it's so easy to bring our own set of assumptions and preconceived ideas. We all have our unique lenses, shaped by our experiences, values, and beliefs, that influence how we see the world. Without even realising it, we often approach situations with our minds already made up, thinking we know what the other person is going to say or how things will unfold. This limits our ability to truly listen and understand the other person's perspective, and it can lead to unnecessary tension or misunderstandings.

But if we can go into conversations with an open mind, willing to genuinely hear new information, it changes everything. It's about setting aside the filter we normally use and being open to the possibility that we don't have all the answers. When we approach discussions this way, we create space for real connection and deeper understanding. This openness is important because it allows for growth, new insights, and sometimes even a shift in perspective. Conversations, especially the tough ones, are opportunities for learning and progress, but only if we're truly open to hearing and considering what the other person has to say.

For example, I once sat in a meeting where a director was giving a performance review to a consultant. The director had based their entire assessment on feedback from another director and accepted it as the absolute truth. No matter how much the consultant tried to explain what had actually happened or provide context, it had already been decided that the consultant's performance was poor. There was no "beginner's mind" — no openness to hearing new information or considering a different perspective.

Putting It All Together

Combining these mindful communication practices — active listening, choosing words wisely, pacing your speech, avoiding assumptions, and practising transparency — creates a more cohesive and collaborative workplace. Imagine a scenario where a project hits a snag. Instead of frustration building, you use active listening to ensure everyone feels heard, reflective listening to validate concerns, and open-ended questions to explore solutions. This mindful approach turns a potentially stressful situation into an opportunity for problem-solving, communication and innovation.

Mindful communication doesn't stop with words. Your body language, eye contact, and facial expressions also communicate volumes. When you align your verbal and non-verbal communication, your message comes across with greater clarity and empathy, fostering stronger connections within your team.

Incorporating these practices into your daily professional life requires consistent effort and self-awareness. Start by paying attention to your current communication habits. Are you rushing through conversations? Making assumptions? Gradually implement these changes — slow down your speech, choose your words carefully, and be more transparent. Over time, these small adjustments will significantly improve how you communicate and collaborate with others.

Encouraging feedback from colleagues can help you identify areas for growth. You can continuously refine your communication style by fostering a culture where constructive feedback is valued. Peer reviews or self-assessments can offer insights into your strengths and areas that need improvement.

Ultimately, mindful communication is about more than just exchanging information — it's about building relationships, understanding diverse perspectives, and working together towards common goals. Mastering these skills in high-performance environments like consulting can make the difference between a successful project and a chaotic workplace.

Managing Difficult Conversations

Navigating challenging conversations requires a mindful, emotionally intelligent approach. These discussions can feel like walking a tightrope, but with the right techniques, you can manage emotions, maintain calm, focus on outcomes, and close with compassion. Let's dive into practical strategies for handling these situations gracefully and effectively.

Preparing Emotionally

Going into a difficult conversation without emotional preparation is like facing a storm without an umbrella. Emotional readiness is crucial. One way to prepare is by reflecting on your emotions before the conversation. Ask yourself: Are you feeling frustrated, angry, or anxious? Identifying these feelings can help you manage them, preventing an emotional outburst during the conversation.

Visualisation is another powerful tool. Imagine yourself handling the conversation calmly and effectively. Visualizing a positive outcome reduces anxiety and boosts confidence. Deep breathing exercises are also a simple but effective method to calm your nervous system before the discussion, making it easier to stay composed.

For deeper emotional preparation, consider practising mindfulness meditation. Even a few minutes of mindfulness can increase emotional awareness and self-regulation, helping you stay present during the conversation. Journaling your thoughts beforehand can also clarify your objectives and emotional state, giving you a clearer path forward.

Staying Calm Under Pressure

When emotions run high, staying calm is essential. It's easy to get swept up in the heat of the moment, but remaining level-headed helps you navigate the conversation more effectively. One strategy is to focus on the bigger picture — why is this conversation important? Keeping the end goal in sight helps maintain perspective.

Another great tactic is slowing down the pace of the conversation. Speak slower, pause between points, and allow time for reflection. This not only gives you space to think but also helps de-escalate the situation. When tensions rise, take a deep breath — inhale slowly through your nose and exhale just as slowly. This simple act can instantly calm your mind and body.

Active listening also plays a huge role here. Instead of reacting immediately, focus on listening. When the other person feels heard, it reduces tension naturally, and you gain more clarity on their perspective.

Maintaining Focus on Outcomes

Conversations can easily veer off track, especially when emotions are involved. Keeping the discussion focused on outcomes ensures that it remains productive. Begin by clearly defining the desired goals at the start. Whether resolving a conflict or reaching a decision, having a clear objective helps guide the conversation.

Throughout the discussion, gently steer the conversation back to its purpose. Use phrases like, "Let's focus on finding a solution," to maintain direction. Encouraging the other party to express their goals also fosters a collaborative atmosphere. This mutual understanding can make it easier to find common ground.

If the conversation drifts into unproductive territory, ask guiding questions like, "How does this relate to our main objective?" This helps bring the focus back to the intended outcome and keeps both parties aligned.

Closing with Compassion

Ending a difficult conversation on a compassionate note leaves a positive impression, regardless of the outcome. Acknowledge the other person's feelings, even if you don't agree with their viewpoint. Simple statements like, "I understand this is a challenging situation," can go a long way in softening the conversation.

Before concluding, ensure both parties have had the opportunity to express their concerns fully. Summarise the key points discussed, and any agreements made. This shows that you've been attentive and value the conversation's substance.

Express gratitude for the other person's openness, saying something like, "I appreciate your honesty," or "Thank you for sharing your perspective." This validates the dialogue and leaves the door open for future discussions, even if you haven't reached full agreement this time.

Leaving the door open for future communication is also important. You might say, "Let's revisit this topic next week" or "Feel free to reach out if you have more thoughts." This conveys flexibility and a willingness to continue working towards a solution.

Building Rapport and Trust

Rapport and trust

Rapport and trust are essential in professional environments, and mindful communication is key to building both. Consistency in communication is the foundation of trust. People are more likely to trust someone whose message remains reliable and steady. Think of it like being the colleague who always shows up when promised — consistency makes you dependable. Deliver on your promises, communicate regularly, and follow through on commitments.

Empathetic dialogue

Empathy in dialogue is equally important. Taking time to truly understand a colleague's concerns fosters mutual respect. Imagine a teammate expressing stress about a looming deadline. Rather than brushing it off with a generic "It'll be fine," you could respond with, "I understand how this is stressing you out. Let's figure out how to tackle it together." This not only validates their feelings but strengthens your working relationship.

Celebrate successes

Celebrating successes together builds camaraderie. Whether it's a team lunch or a shoutout in a meeting, acknowledging achievements fosters a positive atmosphere. A "win wall," where team members post their accomplishments, can encourage ongoing recognition and boost morale.

Place of safety

Creating safe spaces for sharing is vital for fostering collaboration and innovation. In environments where people feel comfortable expressing their thoughts without fear of judgment, diverse ideas flourish. To cultivate these spaces, lead by example. Share your thoughts openly, encourage others to do the same, and emphasise the value of diverse perspectives.

Practical Steps for Mindful Communication

1. Emotional Preparation:

   - Reflect on your feelings before a difficult conversation.
   - Visualise handling the discussion calmly.
   - Practice mindfulness or deep breathing exercises to increase self-regulation.

2. Staying Calm Under Pressure:

   - Slow down the conversation when emotions rise.
   - Focus on listening rather than reacting immediately.
   - Take deep breaths to stay composed and reduce stress.

3. Maintaining Focus on Outcomes:

   - Start by defining clear goals for the conversation.
   - Use guiding phrases to keep the discussion on track.
   - Periodically check whether the conversation is moving toward the desired outcomes.

4. Closing with Compassion:

   - Acknowledge the other person's emotions, even if you disagree.
   - Summarise key points and agreements.
   - Express gratitude for their openness and willingness to engage.

5. Building Rapport and Trust:

- Be consistent and reliable in your communication.
- Show empathy and acknowledge others' concerns.
- Celebrate successes, both big and small.
- Create a safe, judgment-free space for sharing diverse perspectives.

Creating a Mindful Communication Culture

Mindful communication isn't just an individual practice — it can shape entire teams. Setting regular check-ins and practising open, honest dialogue fosters a supportive environment. Imagine a daily 10-minute huddle where team members can briefly update each other, ensuring everyone stays aligned and feels heard.

Fostering a mindful communication culture takes continuous effort. Start small by focusing on one area, such as emotional preparation or active listening, and gradually integrate other practices. As these habits become second nature, you'll notice a significant improvement in team dynamics, leading to stronger relationships built on trust and mutual respect.

Incorporating these mindful strategies will transform your approach to difficult conversations and improve the overall communication culture within your team or organisation. By staying emotionally prepared, calm, and focused on outcomes, you can navigate challenging discussions with clarity and compassion, building a workplace where everyone feels valued and understood.

Key Takeaways

Throughout this chapter, we've explored various aspects of mindful communication and its impact on professional relationships and effectiveness. Let's recap the key insights:

Active Listening Skills:

- Practice being fully present in conversations
- Recognize both verbal and non-verbal cues
- Use reflective listening for validation
- Ask open-ended questions to encourage dialogue

Mindful Speech Practices:

- Choose words wisely to convey precise meanings
- Pay attention to pacing and tone of voice
- Avoid making assumptions about others' knowledge or thoughts
- Practice transparency to build trust and openness

Managing Difficult Conversations:

- Prepare emotionally before challenging discussions
- Stay calm under pressure using techniques like deep breathing
- Maintain focus on desired outcomes

- Close conversations with compassion and empathy

Building Rapport and Trust:

- Maintain consistency in communication
- Show empathy in dialogue
- Celebrate successes together
- Create safe spaces for sharing ideas and concerns

Key takeaways:

- Mindful communication enhances clarity, understanding, and collaboration in professional settings
- Active listening and thoughtful speech are essential for building strong relationships
- Preparing for and managing difficult conversations with mindfulness can lead to better outcomes
- Consistent, empathetic, and transparent communication fosters trust and rapport among team members

Integrating these mindful communication practices into your professional life can significantly improve your interactions, build stronger relationships, and create a more positive and productive work environment. Remember, mindful communication is an ongoing practice that requires consistent effort and self-awareness.

As you move forward, consider which strategies resonate most with you and start incorporating them into your daily communication. With time and practice, you'll likely notice a profound impact on your professional relationships, team dynamics, and overall effectiveness in your high-pressure career.

Chapter 9: Mindful Leadership

Daring leaders work to make sure people can be themselves and feel a sense of belonging.

— *Brené Brown*

Mindful leadership is all about leading with a calm, clear mind and a compassionate attitude. Picture yourself steering a ship through stormy seas, maintaining composure as chaos swirls around you — that's the essence of mindful leadership. In this chapter, we'll explore how mindfulness transforms leadership, enhancing the leader and the entire team dynamic.

We'll delve into key traits of a mindful leader, including self-awareness, empathy, adaptability, and decisiveness. These traits act like leadership superpowers, enabling leaders to face challenges with grace and insight. By embracing self-awareness, leaders can engage more authentically with their teams, fostering an environment built on mutual respect. Empathy takes centre stage, as understanding and valuing team members' perspectives fosters a culture of compassion and collaboration. We'll also explore how adaptability keeps a team agile in the face of constant change and how decisiveness, when paired with mindfulness, turns decision-making into a thoughtful, transparent process. So, get ready for a reflective journey through the nuanced world of mindful leadership, and discover how these qualities can lead to a more harmonious and effective way of guiding and inspiring others.

Traits of a Mindful Leader

Mindful leaders stand out through their self-awareness, empathy, adaptability, and decisiveness. These traits enhance team performance and boost morale, steering the organisation toward success with compassion and efficiency.

Self-awareness is the foundation of mindful leadership. Leaders who regularly reflect on their behaviours, strengths, and weaknesses are better equipped to engage authentically with their teams. This authenticity creates deeper connections and fosters mutual respect. For example, leaders who realise they tend to micromanage can work on delegating tasks more effectively, empowering their team. This shift builds trust and motivation within the team, boosting productivity and overall morale. Leaders who demonstrate vulnerability encourage others to follow suit, creating a culture of openness and trust.

Empathy is another hallmark of mindful leadership. It's not just about understanding your team's needs — it's about feeling them. Actively listening and valuing your team members' input cultivates a culture of compassion and collaboration. For instance, if a team member struggles due to personal issues, an empathetic leader might offer flexibility or additional support. This small act of kindness improves the individual's performance and demonstrates to the team that their well-being is a priority. Empathy helps dismantle hierarchies, fostering a more inclusive and supportive workplace.

Adaptability keeps a team agile in the face of constant change. Mindfulness equips leaders with the mental flexibility to pivot quickly and effectively, whether adjusting strategies in a crisis or embracing new technologies. Adaptable leaders create resilient teams that thrive in dynamic environments.

When combined with mindfulness, decisiveness transforms decision-making from a rushed process into a careful, thoughtful one. Mindful leaders consider multiple perspectives before making decisions, which builds trust and confidence within the team. Imagine a scenario where a company must choose between two significant projects. A mindful leader would gather input from all stakeholders, evaluate the potential impacts, and clearly communicate the decision and rationale. This process ensures the best choice is made and fosters a sense of inclusion and shared purpose within the team.

These traits — self-awareness, empathy, adaptability, and decisiveness — ripple outward, shaping a positive organisational culture. When leaders embody these qualities, they inspire their teams to adopt similar behaviours, creating an environment where open communication, mutual respect, and genuine collaboration thrive. Employees in such environments are more engaged, productive, and committed to the organisation's vision.

For example, an organisation led by a mindful leader might see lower turnover rates and higher employee satisfaction. Employees are more likely to remain engaged when they feel heard and understood. Self-aware leaders avoid ego-driven decisions, making room for balanced, well-considered actions. Empathy bridges gaps, fostering teamwork and collective problem-solving. Adaptability keeps the team resilient amid industry disruptions, while decisiveness brings clarity and direction.

Moreover, companies with mindful leaders often report higher levels of innovation. Creativity flourishes when leaders create safe spaces for sharing ideas without fear of judgment. Employees feel empowered to take risks and explore new avenues, driving the organisation forward. Mindful decision-making leads to better business outcomes, balancing short-term gains with long-term sustainability.

Encouraging Mindfulness Within Teams

Mindful leadership isn't just about personal growth; it's about creating a ripple effect that enhances team performance and well-being. Leaders can encourage mindfulness in their teams by implementing simple yet powerful strategies.

Start by organising workshops and training sessions dedicated to mindfulness. These sessions provide a platform for team members to learn techniques like deep-breathing exercises, meditation, and mindful listening. By making mindfulness part of regular training, leaders can embed these practices into the team's daily routine. These workshops also create a shared language around mindfulness, enabling team members to communicate more effectively about their challenges and experiences.

Creating a mindful workplace culture begins with leaders exemplifying mindfulness in their actions. When leaders remain calm under pressure, practice active listening, and show empathy, they set a powerful example for the team. Highlighting success stories that demonstrate the benefits of mindfulness reinforces its value. Additionally, integrating mindfulness into the organisation's values — through mission statements, team meetings, and performance reviews — ensures it becomes part of the company's DNA.

Another effective strategy is fostering collaborative mindfulness practices. Group meditations, mindfulness exercises, or even short mindfulness breaks during meetings can create a sense of unity and collective awareness. For example, starting or ending meetings with a few minutes of guided meditation promotes calm and focus. These practices not only enhance individual well-being but also strengthen the team dynamic, fostering resilience and mutual support.

Feedback mechanisms are essential for maintaining and improving mindfulness initiatives. Leaders should create formal and informal channels for team members to share their experiences and suggestions. Surveys, feedback forms, and open discussions provide valuable insights into what's working and what needs adjustment. Regular mindfulness check-ins during one-on-one meetings can also offer personalised support and guidance.

Decision-Making with Clarity and Empathy

Mindful decision-making is like having a mental superpower. It involves being fully aware of the present moment, considering various perspectives, and balancing logic with empathy.

Mindful analysis means taking a step back to assess a situation thoroughly before making a decision. This isn't about overthinking but about ensuring all angles are considered. By practising mindful analysis, leaders can make well-informed decisions that benefit the organisation and the team. Taking a thoughtful pause allows leaders to consider facts, feelings, and potential outcomes, leading to wiser, more strategic decisions.

Empathy plays a key role in mindful decision-making. Leaders who practice empathy can see beyond their own viewpoints and understand the concerns of their team members. This empathy fosters trust and strengthens relationships. For example, when implementing a policy change, a mindful leader would engage with the team, understand their concerns, and adjust the plan accordingly. This approach fosters collaboration and ensures that decisions are made with the organisation's goals and the team's well-being in mind.

Clear and transparent communication is critical in decision-making. Mindful leaders explain the reasoning behind their decisions, ensuring everyone understands the 'why' and the 'what.' This transparency builds trust and reduces resistance. By clearly articulating the decision-making process, leaders foster alignment and create a more cohesive team.

Lastly, mindful leaders employ a holistic decision framework, weighing long-term impacts alongside short-term gains. This approach ensures that decisions are sustainable and benefit the organisation in the long run. For example, when faced with budget cuts, a mindful leader might consider alternative cost-saving measures that don't compromise team morale or the company's future growth.

Mindful leadership is about leading with intention, clarity, and compassion. Leaders can create positive, productive workplaces where teams thrive by embodying self-awareness, empathy, adaptability, and decisiveness. Leaders can drive innovation, boost morale, and lead purposefully through mindful decision-making, fostering mindfulness within teams, and encouraging open communication. Integrating mindfulness into your leadership style isn't just a personal transformation — it's a way to inspire lasting, positive change within your organisation.

Leading by Example: Personal Practices

Mindful leadership goes beyond managing tasks — it's about creating a work environment where everyone feels valued, respected, and motivated. Here's how mindful leaders can inspire their teams through personal mindfulness practices.

Modelling Mindfulness

Practising mindfulness openly within your team is like planting seeds of calm and focus in the workplace garden. When leaders regularly demonstrate mindfulness, it sends a clear message: mindfulness is important, and it works. Imagine starting meetings with a brief moment of silence or guided deep breathing exercises. At first, it might feel awkward, but over time, these pauses become a welcome, refreshing moment that helps centre the team. Incorporating mindfulness into your daily routine showcases its benefits and helps create an atmosphere where mindfulness becomes a shared priority.

For example, during high-stress periods like quarterly reviews or tight project deadlines, taking a few moments for mindful breathing can significantly reduce anxiety levels. Not only does this calm the mind, but it also promotes more thoughtful decision-making. By leading in this way, you demonstrate the value of mindfulness in action, and your team is likely to follow your example, leading to a collective improvement in stress management and productivity.

Commitment to Growth

Mindfulness, like any growth-oriented practice, is an ongoing journey. Leaders who commit to their personal development, especially in mindfulness, demonstrate a growth mindset that can be truly inspiring. Whether attending mindfulness workshops, participating in retreats, or reading about the latest mindfulness techniques, showing that you are continually learning sets a powerful example for your team.

Imagine a leader who regularly shares insights from a mindfulness seminar or discusses new techniques they've recently learned. This promotes personal growth and encourages team members to pursue their own growth paths. It fosters a learning culture where everyone is motivated to improve themselves, resulting in a more skilled and resilient team. Your dedication to mindfulness can inspire others to adopt a similar approach to personal and professional development.

Balancing Personal and Professional Life

Effective leadership involves balancing personal well-being with professional responsibilities. Leaders who prioritise self-care send a clear message to their team: it's possible — and necessary — to maintain this balance to avoid burnout. This doesn't just mean taking regular vacations or breaks but integrating self-care into daily routines.

Openly discussing your self-care habits with your team can have a positive ripple effect. Perhaps you practice yoga in the mornings, take walks during lunch, or meditate before starting your workday. Sharing these routines emphasises the importance of maintaining mental and physical health, encouraging your team members to discover their balance. A leader prioritising self-care often finds that their team becomes happier, healthier, and more productive as they see their well-being valued.

Sharing Mindfulness Tools

Providing your team with accessible resources and tools to support their mindfulness practices empowers them to fully engage with mindfulness. This can include recommending meditation or relaxation apps, organising mindfulness workshops, or sharing helpful content like books, articles, and podcasts. Creating a "mindfulness library" with these resources can further support the team's efforts.

Fostering a supportive environment where team members feel comfortable discussing their mindfulness practices can also deepen engagement. Encouraging open conversations about which techniques work for different individuals can lead to the discovery of diverse, effective strategies that benefit the entire team. Sharing these tools and fostering a community of mindful practice can make mindfulness a natural and integral part of the workplace culture.

Leaders can cultivate a mindful workplace by modelling mindfulness, committing to growth, balancing personal and professional life, and sharing helpful tools. Through these practices, leaders inspire their teams to prioritise well-being, manage stress, and stay focused, leading to a more harmonious, productive, and resilient organisation.

Key Takeaways

In this chapter, we've explored mindful leadership's transformative impact on individual leaders and their teams. Let's recap the key insights:

- Traits of a Mindful Leader:
    - Self-awareness: Enables authentic engagement and fosters trust
    - Empathy: Cultivates compassion and improves team dynamics
    - Adaptability: Keeps teams agile in the face of change
    - Decisiveness: Leads to transparent and thoughtful decision-making
- Encouraging Mindfulness Within Teams:
    - Implement workshops and training sessions on mindfulness

- Create a mindful workplace culture by leading by example
- Introduce collaborative mindfulness practices
- Establish feedback mechanisms to continually improve mindfulness initiatives
- Decision-Making with Clarity and Empathy:
    - Practice mindful analysis for well-informed decisions
    - Balance organisational needs with team members' concerns
    - Communicate decision rationale clearly and transparently
    - Adopt a holistic decision framework considering long-term impacts
- Leading by Example: Personal Practices:
    - Model mindfulness openly in daily activities
    - Demonstrate commitment to personal growth and learning
    - Balance personal well-being with professional responsibilities
    - Share mindfulness tools and resources with the team

Key takeaways:

- Mindful leadership enhances team performance, boosts morale, and fosters a positive organisational culture.

- Integrating mindfulness practices into leadership can lead to better decision-making, improved communication, and increased empathy.
- Leaders who prioritise their mindfulness journey inspire their teams to do the same.

A mindful approach to leadership can result in more engaged, productive, and resilient teams.

By embracing mindful leadership principles, leaders can create a work environment that values productivity and the well-being and growth of each team member. This approach leads to stronger team dynamics, enhanced problem-solving capabilities, and a more harmonious workplace culture.

As you move forward in your leadership journey, consider how to incorporate these mindful practices into your daily routines and decision-making processes. Remember, mindful leadership is an ongoing practice that requires consistent effort and self-reflection. With time and dedication, you'll likely see profound changes in your leadership effectiveness and your team's overall success.

Chapter 10: Embracing Mindfulness - Your Path to Professional Excellence

The journey doesn't end here. It's just another path, one we all must take. The road goes ever on and on."

— J.R.R. Tolkien

As we embark on the next phase of our journey of bringing mindfulness into our professional lives, let's take a moment to pull together the key lessons and strategies we've covered. As we've discovered, mindfulness is far more than a passing trend; it's a powerful tool for enhancing workplace performance, resilience, and emotional well-being. Now, we will weave together the threads of mindfulness, reflecting on its practical applications and how it can transform your professional life.

The Mindfulness Advantage

We started by debunking the myth that mindfulness is just a trendy buzzword. In fact, mindfulness is a scientifically validated practice that profoundly affects mental and emotional health. The neuroscience behind mindfulness reveals its capacity to reshape the brain, enhancing regions responsible for focus, emotional regulation, and decision-making. This neuroplasticity is the cornerstone of developing resilience in professional challenges.

In the high-pressure business world, mindfulness is an anchor, keeping us grounded in the present moment. It enables us to respond thoughtfully rather than react impulsively when stress or complexity arises. This shift from reactivity to responsiveness is a crucial skill in today's fast-paced, demanding work environments.

Integrating Mindfulness into Your Professional Toolkit

Mindfulness is not a one-size-fits-all solution but a flexible set of practices you can tailor to fit your unique needs. From simple breath awareness exercises you can do during a hectic workday to more structured meditation practices, the key is finding what resonates with you and making it a consistent part of your routine.

It's important to remember that mindfulness isn't about eliminating stress or achieving a state of perpetual calm. Rather, it's about developing a balanced relationship with your thoughts, emotions, and the challenges you face. It builds your capacity to stay centred and focused, even when the world around you is in flux.

The Ripple Effect of Mindful Leadership

Mindfulness isn't just a personal practice; when embraced by leaders, it can transform entire organisational cultures. We've seen how mindful leaders — characterised by self-awareness, empathy, adaptability, and thoughtful decision-making — create environments where creativity thrives, communication flows, and team members feel valued and heard.

Leaders who model mindfulness inspire their teams to follow suit. You don't need a formal leadership title to make a difference. We can influence the culture around us by embodying mindfulness in our interactions and work habits. Whether you are a team leader or a member, you can help create a more mindful, collaborative, and effective workplace.

Emotional Intelligence and Resilience

A significant part of our mindfulness journey involved building emotional resilience. By understanding emotional triggers and developing mindful strategies to manage them, we can navigate professional challenges more easily and effectively.

Techniques like reflection, body scanning, and mindful breathing serve as tools for emotional regulation, enabling us to maintain composure and clarity during stressful situations. This emotional intelligence, cultivated through mindfulness, is invaluable in managing interpersonal dynamics, resolving conflicts, and staying motivated through setbacks.

The Art of Mindful Communication

Mindfulness also profoundly impacts communication. By practising active listening, speaking with intention, and being fully present during interactions, we can strengthen professional relationships, avoid misunderstandings, and collaborate more effectively.

Mindful communication isn't just about the words we use; it also involves recognising non-verbal cues and being aware of the emotional currents in conversations. This heightened awareness helps us navigate difficult conversations with empathy and skill, turning potential conflicts into opportunities for growth and understanding.

Decision-Making with Clarity

Mindfulness transforms decision-making from a hurried, stress-driven process into one that is thoughtful and deliberate. By pausing to reflect before acting, we make decisions aligned with our values and long-term goals rather than being swayed by short-term pressures or emotions.

Mindful decision-making considers multiple perspectives and anticipates potential outcomes. It fosters a more ethical, balanced approach, benefiting the decision-maker and the entire team or organisation. This reflective practice leads to smarter, more sustainable decisions.

Fostering a Mindful Organisational Culture

While individual mindfulness practices are powerful, their impact multiplies when integrated into a broader organisational culture. Creating a mindful workplace goes beyond offering meditation classes or wellness workshops. It fosters an environment where reflection is valued, communication is open, and employee well-being is prioritised.

Leaders play a pivotal role in shaping this culture, but every team member can contribute to fostering a mindful ethos. By championing mindfulness in your daily professional interactions, you become an agent of positive change, subtly influencing the culture of your workplace.

The Power of Commitment

As you embark on your journey to integrate mindfulness into your professional life, remember that the most significant changes often stem from small, consistent actions taken over time. Each mindful breath, each moment of presence, and every moment of compassion are steps toward building a more fulfilling and effective career. The modern workplace may never be free from challenges, but cultivating mindfulness equips you with an invaluable inner resource to face whatever comes your way.

You're enhancing your well-being and professional performance and contributing to a larger movement towards more mindful, human-centred workplaces. Imagine a world where decisions are made with clarity and compassion, communication is defined by deep listening and mutual understanding, and challenges are met with resilience and creativity. This is the potential of mindfulness, and it begins with each of us committing to this practice.

As you conclude this book, take a moment to reflect on your intentions. What aspect of mindfulness resonates most strongly with you? Which step will you take first to incorporate mindfulness into your workday? Remember, the journey of a thousand miles begins with a single step. Your mindful step today can be the start of a profound transformation in your professional and personal life.

The world of work is evolving rapidly, and the professionals who succeed will be those who can maintain focus, adapt to change, and navigate complex human dynamics with skill and compassion. By embracing mindfulness, you're not only preparing yourself for the future of work; you're actively shaping it. You are becoming a part of the movement that defines a new, mindful approach to leadership and collaboration.

Take a deep breath, ground yourself in this moment, and step forward into your mindful professional journey. The path ahead is filled with possibility, and with each mindful step, you are creating a more fulfilling, effective, and meaningful professional life. The time to begin is now.

The Journey Ahead: A Call to Action

As we wrap up this exploration of mindfulness in the professional world, we must recognise that this is just the beginning. Applying these insights and practices in your daily life is the real challenge. Here's a roadmap to guide your next steps:

- Start Small, But Start Now: Incorporate one mindfulness practice into your routine. Whether it's taking three mindful breaths before a meeting or practising a brief body scan during breaks, the key is consistency over the duration.
- Cultivate Self-Awareness: Commit to regular self-reflection. Keeping a journal of your emotional responses to work situations can help identify patterns and triggers. Awareness is the first step toward meaningful change.
- Prioritise Well-Being: Self-care is essential for sustainable success. Schedule activities that nourish your mind and body, whether meditation, exercise, or a hobby you love.
- Practice Mindful Communication: In your next conversation, focus on being fully present, actively listening, and speaking with intention. Notice how these small changes enhance the quality of your interactions.

- Embrace a Growth Mindset: Approach challenges with curiosity rather than frustration. Use mindfulness to navigate difficulties as opportunities for growth.
- Share Your Journey: As you experience the benefits of mindfulness, share your insights with colleagues. Consider starting a mindfulness group or suggesting mindful practices for team meetings.
- Seek Continuous Learning: Stay curious and explore new mindfulness practices. Attend workshops, read books, or go on retreats to deepen your practice.
- Be Patient and Compassionate with Yourself: Mindfulness is a lifelong journey. Some days will be challenging, and that's okay. Treat yourself with kindness and start again.
- Integrate Mindfulness into Decision-Making: Before making important decisions, pause to reflect. Consider the broader implications and ensure your choices align with your values.
- Lead by Example: Whether you're in a formal leadership role, embody the principles of mindfulness. Your actions and attitudes can inspire others and contribute to a more mindful workplace culture.
- Commit to the journey: Committing to the journey of mindfulness is about embracing small, consistent practices that lead to profound personal and professional transformation over time.

Mindfulness offers a path to greater clarity, resilience, and success in professional life. By integrating mindful practices into your daily routine, you equip yourself with tools to navigate challenges with grace, build stronger relationships, and make more thoughtful decisions. As you move forward, remember that mindfulness is not a destination but a journey that will enrich your personal and professional life, helping you become the best version of yourself.

Final words

I want to express my deepest gratitude. Thank you for taking the time to read this book and for allowing me to share my thoughts and insights, practices, and tools that can transform your personal and professional life, as they have done with mine. With countless options out there, your choice to read this one means a lot to me, and I truly appreciate you making it to the end.

I sincerely hope that you've found real value in these pages and that the principles of mindfulness resonate with you in a way that will positively shape the path ahead.

I firmly believe that embracing a mindful approach will make a huge difference, not only in how you navigate challenges but in how you experience success, fulfilment, and balance. The secrets to this journey are simple but profound: having a clear intention, committing fully to the practice, and, most importantly, being patient and compassionate with yourself.

Remember, this is a marathon, not a sprint. True, lasting change takes time, but the rewards will be worth it with consistency.

Before you leave, I have a small request: would you consider posting a review on the platform? Reviews are one of the best ways to support independent authors like me. Your insights will help me continue writing the kinds of books that resonate with you. I'd love to hear your thoughts!

I wish you all the success as you step into the future with mindfulness as your guide. May your journey be one of growth, resilience, and endless possibility.

The best is yet to come.

Sources

Chapter 1

Ackerman, C. (2017, January 18). 22 mindfulness exercises, techniques; activities for adults (+ pdf's). Positive Psychology. https://positivepsychology.com/mindfulness-exercises-techniques-activities/

Bostock, S., Crosswell, A. D., Prather, A. A.; Steptoe, A. (2019, February). Mindfulness on-the-go: Effects of a mindfulness meditation app on work stress and well-being. Journal of Occupational Health Psychology. https://doi.org/10.1037/ocp0000118

Boyce, B. (2020, February 20). Where Does the Path of Mindfulness Lead? Mindful. https://www.mindful.org/where-does-the-path-of-mindfulness-lead/

Dweck, C.S. (2006). Mindset: The new psychology of success. New York: Random House

Goldstein, E., Topitzes, J., Brown, R. L., Barrett, B. (2018, May 7). Mediational pathways of meditation and exercise on mental health and perceived stress: A randomized controlled trial. Journal of Health Psychology. https://doi.org/10.1177/1359105318772608

Hölzel, B.K., Carmody, J., Vangel, M., Congleton, C., Yerramsetti, S.M., Gard, T., & Lazar, S.W. (2011).

Mindfulness practice leads to increases in regional brain grey matter density. Psychiatry Research: Neuroimaging, 191(1), pp.36-43.

Johnson, D.C., Thom, N.J., Stanley, E.A., Haase, L., Simmons, A.N., Shih, P.A., Thompson, W.K., & Paulus, M.P. (2014). Modifying resilience mechanisms in at-risk individuals: A controlled study of mindfulness training in Marines preparing for deployment. American Journal of Psychiatry, 171(8), pp.844-853.

Klein, J.T., Kuhlmann, T., & Roeser, R.W. (2021). Mindfulness and resilience in the military: Exploring the impact of a mindfulness training program on psychological resilience in Navy SEALs. Mindfulness, 12(1), pp.45-58.

Kriakous, S. A., Elliott, K. A., Lamers, C.,; Owen, R. (2020, September 24). The Effectiveness of mindfulness-based Stress Reduction on the Psychological Functioning of Healthcare professionals: a Systematic Review. Mindfulness. https://doi.org/10.1007/s12671-020-01500-9

Milly. (2024, May 9). Healing And Growth Made Simple: A Roadmap. The Opinionated Magpies. https://theopinionatedmagpies.com/healing-and-growth-made-simple/

Peck, M. S. (1978). The Road Less Traveled: A New Psychology of Love, Traditional Values and Spiritual Growth. Simon & Schuster.

Schmidt, S., Schwencke, C., & Andersson, G. (2020). Mindfulness training in military personnel and veterans: A systematic review and meta-analysis. Journal of Clinical Psychology, 76(5), pp.867-885.

Selva, J. (2017, March 13). History of Mindfulness: from East to West and Religion to Science. PositivePsychology.com. https://positivepsychology.com/history-of-mindfulness/

Singh, S. P. (2023, April). Sakshi and Dhyana: the origin of mindfulness-based therapies. BJPsych Bulletin. https://doi.org/10.1192/bjb.2022.39

Taren, A.A., Creswell, J.D., & Gianaros, P.J. (2013). Altered stress-related brain connectivity after mindfulness meditation. NeuroImage, 82, pp.52-60.

Chapter 2

Chiesa, A., Calati, R.,; Serretti, A. (2011, April). Does mindfulness training improve cognitive abilities? A systematic review of neuropsychological findings. Clinical Psychology Review. https://doi.org/10.1016/j.cpr.2010.11.003

Congleton, C., Hölzel, B. K.,; Lazar, S. W. (2015, January 8). Mindfulness can literally change your brain. Harvard Business Review. https://hbr.org/2015/01/mindfulness-can-literally-change-your-brain

Davis, D. M.,; Hayes, J. A. (2012, July). What are the benefits of mindfulness? American Psychological Association. https://www.apa.org/monitor/2012/07-08/ce-corner

Hölzel, B.K., Carmody, J., Vangel, M., Congleton, C., Yerramsetti, S.M., Gard, T., & Lazar, S.W. (2011). Mindfulness practice leads to increases in regional brain gray matter density. Psychiatry Research: Neuroimaging, 191(1), pp.36-43.

Janssen, M., Heerkens, Y., Kuijer, W., van der Heijden, B.,; Engels, J. (2018, January 24). Effects of Mindfulness-Based Stress Reduction on employees' mental health: A systematic review (K. Ebmeier, Ed.). PLOS ONE. https://doi.org/10.1371/journal.pone.0191332

Jiménez-Picón, N., Romero-Martín, M., Ponce-Blandón, J. A., Ramirez-Baena, L., Palomo-Lara, J. C.,; Gómez-Salgado, J. (2021, May 20). The Relationship between Mindfulness and Emotional Intelligence as a Protective Factor for Healthcare Professionals: Systematic Review. International Journal of Environmental Research and Public Health. https://doi.org/10.3390/ijerph18105491

Rogerson, O., Wilding, S., Prudenzi, A.,; O'Connor, D. B. (2023, October 1). Effectiveness of stress management interventions to change cortisol levels: a systematic review and meta-analysis. Psychoneuroendocrinology; Elsevier BV. https://doi.org/10.1016/j.psyneuen.2023.106415

Schuman-Olivier, Z., Trombka, M., Lovas, D. A., Brewer, J. A., Vago, D. R., Gawande, R., Dunne, J. P., Lazar, S. W., Loucks, E. B.,; Fulwiler, C. (2020). Mindfulness and behavior change. Harvard Review of Psychiatry. https://doi.org/10.1097/HRP.0000000000000277

Wimmer, L., Bellingrath, S.,; von Stockhausen, L. (2016, July 12). Cognitive Effects of Mindfulness Training: Results of a Pilot Study Based on a Theory Driven Approach. Frontiers in Psychology. https://doi.org/10.3389/fpsyg.2016.01037

Chapter 3

Arnsten, A.F., 2009. Stress signalling pathways that impair prefrontal cortex structure and function. Nature reviews neuroscience, 10(6), pp.410-422.

Davidson, R.J., Lutz, A. and Ricard, M., 2004. Meditation and the neuroscience of consciousness: An introduction. Cognition, 94(1), pp.47-53.

Fink, A. and Neubauer, A.C., 2006. EEG alpha oscillations during the performance of verbal creativity tasks: Differential effects of sex and verbal intelligence. International Journal of Psychophysiology, 62(1), pp.46-53.

Gerritsen, R.J. and Band, G.P., 2018. Breath of life: the respiratory vagal stimulation model of contemplative activity. Frontiers in human neuroscience, 12, p.397.

Good, D.J., Lyddy, C.J., Glomb, T.M., Bono, J.E., Brown, K.W., Duffy, M.K., Baer, R.A., Brewer, J.A. and Lazar, S.W., 2016. Contemplating mindfulness at work: An integrative review. Journal of management, 42(1), pp.114-142.

Lomas, T., Ivtzan, I. and Fu, C.H., 2015. A systematic review of the neurophysiology of mindfulness on EEG oscillations. Neuroscience & Biobehavioral Reviews, 57, pp.401-410.

Tang, Y.Y., Hölzel, B.K. and Posner, M.I., 2015. The neuroscience of mindfulness meditation. Nature Reviews Neuroscience, 16(4), pp.213-225.

Vogel, S. and Schwabe, L., 2016. Learning and memory under stress: implications for the classroom. npj Science of Learning, 1(1), pp.1-10.

Chapters 4 and 5

ACE Fitness. (2023, September 5). 6 Breathing Exercises to Reduce Stress. Acefitness.org. https://www.acefitness.org/resources/pros/expert-articles/6014/6-breathing-exercises-to-reduce-stress/

Ankrom, S. (2024, February 16). Need a Breather? Try These 9 Breathing Exercises to Relieve Anxiety. Verywell Mind. https://www.verywellmind.com/abdominal-breathing-2584115

Csikszentmihalyi, M. (1990). Flow: The psychology of optimal experience. Harper & Row.

De Couck, M., Caers, R., Musch, L., Fliegauf, J., Giangreco, A.,; Gidron, Y. (2019, May). How breathing can help you make better decisions: Two studies on the effects of breathing patterns on heart rate variability and decision-making in business cases. International Journal of Psychophysiology. https://doi.org/10.1016/j.ijpsycho.2019.02.011

Jerath, R., Edry, J. W., Barnes, V. A., & Jerath, V. (2006). Physiology of long pranayamic breathing: Neural respiratory elements may provide a mechanism that explains how slow deep breathing shifts the autonomic nervous system. Medical Hypotheses, 67(3), 566-571.

Mayo Clinic Staff. (2020, September 15). Mindfulness exercises. Mayo Clinic. https://www.mayoclinic.org/healthy-lifestyle/consumer-health/in-depth/mindfulness-exercises/art-20046356

National Institutes of Health. (2021). Mindfulness for your health. NIH News in Health. https://newsinhealth.nih.gov/2021/06/mindfulness-your-health

Relaxation Techniques for Stress Relief - HelpGuide.org. (2018, October 23). HelpGuide.org. https://www.helpguide.org/mental-health/stress/relaxation-techniques-for-stress-relief

Stinson, A. (2018, June 1). Box breathing: How to do it, benefits, and tips. Www.medicalnewstoday.com. https://www.medicalnewstoday.com/articles/321805

Zaccaro, A., Piarulli, A., Laurino, M., Garbella, E., Menicucci, D., Neri, B.,; Gemignani, A. (2018, September 7). How breath-control can change your life: A systematic review on psycho-physiological correlates of slow breathing. Frontiers in Human Neuroscience. https://doi.org/10.3389/fnhum.2018.00353

Chapter 6

Behan, C. (2020, May 14). The benefits of meditation and mindfulness practices during times of crisis such as covid-19. Irish Journal of Psychological Medicine. https://doi.org/10.1017/ipm.2020.38

Getting Started with Mindfulness. (2018). Mindful. https://www.mindful.org/meditation/mindfulness-getting-started/

Mayo Clinic. (2023, December 14). Meditation: A simple, fast way to reduce stress. Mayo Clinic. https://www.mayoclinic.org/tests-procedures/meditation/in-depth/meditation/art-20045858

Mindful. (2019, April 13). How to meditate. Mindful. https://www.mindful.org/how-to-meditate/

Mindfulness Meditation: Types, Strategies and Benefits | Bloomington Meadows Hospital. (2024, June 10). Bloomington Meadows Hospital | Official Website. https://www.bloomingtonmeadows.com/blog/mindfulness-meditation-types-strategies-benefits/

Raypole, C. (2020, March 26). Body Scan Meditation: Benefits and How to Do It. Healthline. https://www.healthline.com/health/body-scan-meditation

Scott, E. (2024, February 12). What is body scan meditation? Verywell Mind. https://www.verywellmind.com/body-scan-meditation-why-and-how-3144782

Watson, T., Walker, O., Cann, R.,; Varghese, A. K. (2022, January 31). The benefits of mindfulness in mental healthcare professionals. F1000Research. https://doi.org/10.12688/f1000research.73729.2

Chapter 7

Baikie, K.A. and Wilhelm, K., 2005. Emotional and physical health benefits of expressive writing. Advances in Psychiatric Treatment, 11(5), pp.338-346.

Cheng, S.T., Tsui, P.K. and Lam, J.H., 2015. Improving mental health in health care practitioners: Randomized controlled trial of a gratitude intervention. Journal of Consulting and Clinical Psychology, 83(1), pp.177-186.

Chowdhury, M. R. (2019, August 13). Emotional regulation: 6 key skills to regulate emotions. Positive Psychology. https://positivepsychology.com/emotion-regulation/

Cooks-Campbell, A. (2022, July 15). Triggers: Learn to Recognize and Deal with Them. BetterUp. https://www.betterup.com/blog/triggers

Craig, H. (2019, January 16). Resilience in the Workplace: How to be More Resilient at Work. PositivePsychology.com. https://positivepsychology.com/resilience-in-the-workplace/

Crego, A., Yela, J. R., Riesco-Matías, P., Gómez-Martínez, M.-Á.,; Vicente-Arruebarrena, A. (2022). The Benefits of Self-Compassion in Mental Health Professionals: A Systematic Review of Empirical Research. Psychology Research and Behavior Management. https://doi.org/10.2147/PRBM.S359382

Emmons, R.A. and McCullough, M.E., 2003. Counting blessings versus burdens: An experimental investigation of gratitude and subjective well-being in daily life. Journal of Personality and Social Psychology, 84(2), pp.377-389.

Garcia, A. C. M., Ferreira, A. C. G., Silva, L. S. R., da Conceição, V. M., Nogueira, D. A.,; Mills, J. (2022, March). Mindful self-care, self-compassion, and resilience among palliative care providers during the COVID-19 pandemic.

Journal of Pain and Symptom Management. https://doi.org/10.1016/j.jpainsymman.2022.03.003

Guendelman, S., Medeiros, S.,; Rampes, H. (2017, March 6). Mindfulness and Emotion Regulation: Insights from Neurobiological, Psychological, and Clinical Studies. Frontiers in Psychology. https://doi.org/10.3389/fpsyg.2017.00220

Hasanzadeh, R., Khoshknab, M.F. and Norozi, K., 2014. The effects of journaling on anxiety in women with multiple sclerosis. Chronic Diseases Journal, 2(1), pp.25-31.

Sohal, H., Kim-Godwin, Y. and Gazadinda, G., 2022. Journaling interventions and mental health: A systematic review and meta-analysis. Journal of Mental Health and Well-Being, 34(3), pp.145-160.

Stice, E., Burton, E., Bearman, S.K. and Rohde, P., 2006. Randomised trial of a brief cognitive-behavioral depression prevention program: An evaluation of acute effects, relapse prevention effects, and mediators. Journal of Consulting and Clinical Psychology, 74(2), pp.290-299.

Tonya. (2024, March 18). Identifying Emotional Triggers and Building Resilience with Self-Regulation. Your Aha! Life. https://yourahalife.com/identifying-emotional-triggers-and-building-resilience-with-self-regulation/

Wood, A.M., Joseph, S. and Maltby, J., 2009. Gratitude predicts psychological well-being above the Big Five facets. Personality and Individual Differences, 46(4), pp.443-447.

Wut, T.-M., Lee, S.-W.,; Xu, J. (Bill). (2022, September 19). Role of Organizational Resilience and Psychological Resilience in the Workplace — Internal Stakeholder Perspective. International Journal of Environmental Research and Public Health. https://doi.org/10.3390/ijerph191811799

Chapter 8

Clarity. (2024, August 20). Connected Speech Pathology. Connected Speech Pathology. https://connectedspeechpathology.com/blog/clarity-of-speech-proven-strategies-for-clear-communication

Cuncic, A. (2024). 7 Active listening techniques for better communication. Verywell Mind. https://www.verywellmind.com/what-is-active-listening-3024343

David, S. (2014, June 19). Manage a Difficult Conversation with Emotional Intelligence. Harvard Business Review. https://hbr.org/2014/06/manage-a-difficult-conversation-with-emotional-intelligence

Editor. (2023, July 19). Building Rapport and Trust through Effective Communication [9 Ways].

https://rcademy.com/building-rapport-and-trust-through-effective-communication/

Editors Desk. (2024, May 2). Emotional Intelligence in Difficult Conversations: Navigating Conflict with Compassion and Clarity. Ei-Matters. https://ei-matters.com/emotional-intelligence-in-difficult-conversations-navigating-conflict-with-compassion-and-clarity/

Lansing, A. E., Romero, N. J., Siantz, E., Silva, V., Center, K., Casteel, D.,; Gilmer, T. (2023, June 28). Building trust: Leadership Reflections on Community Empowerment and Engagement in a Large Urban Initiative. BMC Public Health. https://bmcpublichealth.biomedcentral.com/articles/10.1186/s12889-023-15860-z

Mind Tools Content Team. (n.d.). MindTools | Home. Www.mindtools.com. https://www.mindtools.com/af4nwki/mindful-listening

Sharp Emerson, M. (2021, August 30). 8 ways you can improve your communication skills. Professional Development | Harvard DCE. https://professional.dce.harvard.edu/blog/8-ways-you-can-improve-your-communication-skills/

Chapter 9

A Guide to Practicing Self-Care with Mindfulness. (2020, December 18). Mindful. https://www.mindful.org/a-guide-to-practicing-self-care-with-mindfulness/

Editor. (2023, December 23). Interpersonal Skills for Leaders [9 FAQs]. https://rcademy.com/interpersonal-skills-for-leaders/

Stedham, Y.,; Skaar, T. B. (2019, July 10). Mindfulness, Trust, and Leader Effectiveness: A Conceptual Framework. Frontiers in Psychology. https://doi.org/10.3389/fpsyg.2019.01588

What is mindful leadership? 10 ways to lead with mindfulness. (n.d.). Calm Blog. https://www.calm.com/blog/mindful-leadership

Yu, L.,; Zellmer-Bruhn, M. (2019, May 31). What Mindfulness Can Do for a Team. Harvard Business Review. https://hbr.org/2019/05/what-mindfulness-can-do-for-a-team